DK EYEWITNESS

T0001400

TOP **10**
CUBA

Top 10 Cuba Highlights

The Top 10 of Everything

CONTENTS

Cuba Area by Area

Streetsmart

Within each Top 10 list in this book, no hierarchy of quality or popularity is implied. All 10 are, in the editor's opinion, of roughly equal merit.

Throughout this book, floors are referred to in accordance with American usage; i.e., the "first floor" is at ground level.

Title page, front cover and spine *Vintage cars in Havana*
Back cover, clockwise from top left *Fruit stand; Trinidad; Valle de Viñales; Havana; Playa Esmeralda*

The rapid rate at which the world is changing is constantly keeping the DK Eyewitness team on our toes. While we've worked hard to ensure that this edition of Cuba is accurate and up-to-date, we know that opening hours alter, standards shift, prices fluctuate, places close and new ones pop up in their stead. So, if you notice we've got something wrong or left something out, we want to hear about it. Please get in touch at **travelguides@dk.com**

Welcome to
Cuba

With its soaring mountains, beautiful beaches, complex politics, and thrilling music, Cuba is endlessly intriguing. Add the world's best cigars, plus classic cars cruising cities frozen in the 1950s, and it's no wonder this Caribbean island is a hot destination. With DK Eyewitness Top 10 Cuba, it's yours to explore.

Havana – the irrepressible capital city – awes us with its stunning architecture and overwhelming gifts of art, dance, and music. Walking the cobbled streets of **La Habana Vieja** is a journey back through the centuries, while **Vedado** recalls the wealth of a glittering pre-revolutionary heyday. Chock-full of outstanding museums, art galleries, and lively bars, Havana is a world-class city moving to the rhythms of rumba and salsa.

Cuba is a marvelously varied island, from the stunningly beautiful **Valle de Viñales**, where oxen plough tobacco fields, to the gorgeous beaches of **Cayo Coco**. Well-preserved colonial-era cities such as **Trinidad** and **Camagüey** – both UNESCO World Heritage Sites – are cradles of history and culture. In the east, **Santiago de Cuba** is known for its iconic revolutionary sites and a culture that owes much to its predominantly African heritage. Beyond the forest-clad **Sierra Maestra** lies charming **Baracoa**, founded in 1511 and boasting a jaw-dropping setting surrounded by mountains.

Whether you're visiting for a weekend or a week, our Top 10 guide brings the best of everything the country has to offer, from **María la Gorda** in the west to **Punta Maisí** in the east. The guide has useful tips throughout, from seeking out what's free to finding the best private restaurants, plus seven easy-to-follow itineraries designed to tie together a clutch of sights in a short space of time. Add inspiring photography and detailed maps, and you've got the essential pocket-sized travel companion. **Enjoy the book, and enjoy Cuba.**

Clockwise from top: Playa Ancón, Gran Teatro in Havana, divers in María la Gorda, street in Trinidad, Cuban cigars, Ford Fairline car, musicians at La Bodeguita del Medio in Havana

Exploring Cuba

Cuba is home to a remarkable capital city, gorgeous beaches, and colonial towns. Whether you simply want to immerse yourself in Havana or go farther afield, these two- and seven-day itineraries will help you make the most of this fascinating country.

Key
— Two-day itinerary
— Seven-day itinerary

Cayo Guillermo offers white-sand beaches and perfect coral reefs.

Two Days in Havana

Day ❶
MORNING
Hop aboard the **Havana BusTour** *(see p120)* and enjoy an overview sightseeing tour of the entire city. You can leap off at any sight you wish to visit; another bus will be along soon, and it's all covered by one all-day ticket.

AFTERNOON
Visit the Modernist Palace of Fine Arts, part of the **Museo Nacional de Bellas Artes** *(see p74)*, for its remarkable collection of Cuban art, and **Museo de la Revolución** *(see p75)* for a profile on the Revolution. Explore **Parque Central** *(see p75)* and walk **Paseo de Martí** *(see p76)*. End the day with a sunset stroll along the **Malecón** *(see p76)*.

Day ❷
MORNING
Explore the restored colonial plazas of **La Habana Vieja** *(see pp12–13)*, starting with Plaza de Armas and the Plaza de la Catedral.

AFTERNOON
Wander along **Calle Mercaderes** *(see p74)* to reach **Plaza Vieja** *(see p73)*. Charming Calle Brasil then connects you to **Plaza de San Francisco** *(see p74)*, with its magnificent basilica.

Seven Days in Cuba

Days ❶ and ❷
Follow the two-day Havana itinerary.

Day ❸
Visit the **Museo Ernest Hemingway** *(see p76)*, then head east via the **Zapata Peninsula** *(see pp18–19)*,

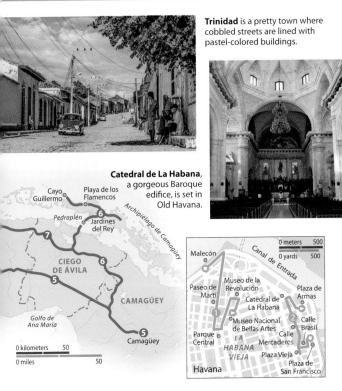

Trinidad is a pretty town where cobbled streets are lined with pastel-colored buildings.

Catedral de La Habana, a gorgeous Baroque edifice, is set in Old Havana.

stopping for lunch before calling at Museo Girón for a history lesson on the Bay of Pigs invasion *(see p41)*. Travel to the port city of **Cienfuegos** *(see p94)* and admire the buildings around Plaza Martí before dinner at the astonishing **Palacio del Valle** *(see p99)*.

Day ❹
Drive to **Trinidad** *(see pp20–21)* to immerse yourself in its architectural beauty as you wander around Plaza Mayor. After lunch, continue exploring Trinidad's cobbled streets. End your day by cooling off at **Playa Ancón** *(see pp104–5)*.

Day ❺
Journey via the scenic **Valle de los Ingenios** *(see p103)* and follow the Carretera Central to the UNESCO World Heritage city of **Camagüey**

(see pp26–7). Admire the city's spruced up historic center, being sure to include charming Plaza del Carmen.

Day ❻
Start early and head across the Pedraplén to the **Jardines del Rey** *(see pp24–5)*. Laze on your choice of glorious beaches and swim in the warm turquoise sea at Cayo Coco's Playa de los Flamencos or on the island of Cayo Guillermo.

Day ❼
Head west to **Remedios** *(see p95)* to savor its colonial ambience, then continue to **Santa Clara** *(see p94)*. Before returning to Havana, view the **Monumento del Che** *(see p39)*, beneath which the remains of celebrated revolutionary Ernesto "Che" Guevara *(see p41)* are interred.

Top 10 Cuba Highlights

Catedral de La Habana, Havana

🔟 Cuba Highlights

Cuba is a land of incredible beauty and amazing contrasts, from white-sand beaches and azure seas to lush valleys and cloud-draped mountains. It is set in a time warp of colonial buildings and pre-revolutionary cars, and its vivacious populace is a blend of Spanish, African, Chinese, and other European peoples.

① La Habana Vieja, Havana

Colonial castles, palaces, and cobbled plazas recall the days when Old Havana was the Americas' richest city *(see pp12–13).*

② The Modern City, Havana

This throbbing metropolis offers museums, parks, beaches, 1950s hotels and nightclubs, and stunning examples of architecture from Beaux Arts to *modernismo (see pp14–15).*

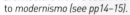

Cordillera de Guaniguanico ③

A few hours west of Havana, these mountains are known for their dramatic rock formations and spectacular caves *(see pp16–17).*

④ Zapata Peninsula

This vast swampland and park protects many endemic bird species, and two museums recall the Bay of Pigs invasion of 1961 *(see pp18–19).*

Trinidad ⑤

Colorful Trinidad enjoys a hillside setting. This lovely UNESCO World Heritage Site is justifiably one of Cuba's most popular cities *(see pp20–21).*

Jardines del Rey ⑥

Stretching 275 miles (442 km) along Cuba's northern coastline, this chain of offshore islands and cays is lined with stunning beaches *(see pp24–5)*.

⑦ Camagüey

The colonial buildings of Camagüey were made a World Heritage Site in 2008, and the city is slowly being restored. It is awash with imposing churches looming over cobbled plazas *(see pp26–7)*.

Holguín ⑧

This provincial capital has played a key role in Cuban history. Its plazas are lined with museums and cultural centers. Castro's birthplace and a beach resort are two nearby attractions *(see pp28–9)*.

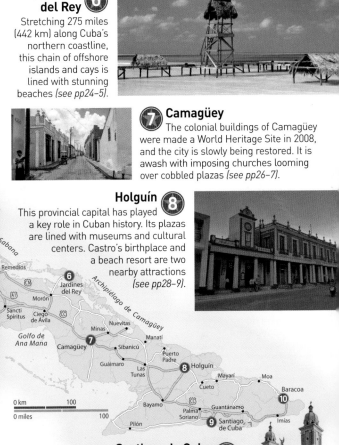

Santiago de Cuba ⑨

Santiago de Cuba exudes a mystique influenced by its French and Afro-Caribbean links. It is home to Cuba's oldest building and a cathedral, plus sites and monuments relating to the Revolution *(see pp30–31)*.

Baracoa ⑩

Cuba's first city, founded in 1511, Baracoa enjoys a stupendous bayside setting backed by rainforest-clad mountains *(see pp32–3)*.

TOP10 ⭐ La Habana Vieja, Havana

With almost 1,000 buildings of historic importance, this intimate quarter is perhaps the largest and most complete colonial complex in the Americas. Old Havana has an astonishing wealth of castles, churches, convents, palaces, and other important buildings spanning five centuries and subject to an ongoing restoration program. Easily walkable, the cobbled plazas and the narrow streets of La Habana Vieja exude charm.

3 Catedral de La Habana

Dominating a cobbled plaza, this cathedral (right) is graced by an exquisite Baroque facade with asymmetrical bell towers. The restored interior features fine murals.

4 Calle Mercaderes

This cobbled street links Calle Obispo to Plaza Vieja. Lined with tiny museums, boutiques, colonial mansions, and other attractions, it offers much to explore *(see p74).*

1 Palacio de los Capitanes Generales

This former governor's palace (above) houses the City Museum. Displays of colonial treasures in lavishly decorated hallways and chambers recall the height of Spanish power.

5 Museo Nacional de Bellas Artes

The fine arts museum is housed in two buildings and displays both an international collection and Cuban art (right) *(see p74).*

2 Basilica Menor de San Francisco de Asís

This basilica, located in Plaza de San Francisco, has a museum and is a venue for concerts.

6 Plaza Vieja

The fountain at the heart of Old Havana's largest plaza (left) is an exact replica of the 17th-century original. Sites to explore here include a brew-pub, a boutique, and intimate museums and galleries *(see p73).*

9 Calle Obispo

This pedestrian-only thoroughfare is lined with book shops, eclectic stores **(left)**, art galleries, bars with live music, and cafés.

THE CITY WALLS

Havana's fortified city walls were completed in 1697 and encircled the original colonial city. The 30-ft- (9-m-) high wall was protected by nine bastions and a moat. However, by the early 19th century the city was bursting at the seams. This rapid expansion led to the eventual tearing down of the city wall in 1863. Today only fragments of the original wall remain.

10 Parque Histórico-Militar Morro-Cabaña

Completed in 1774 as the largest fortress in the Americas, the Cabaña fortress offers dramatic views across the harbor to La Habana Vieja. The Morro castle nearby has a museum and lighthouse.

7 Plaza de Armas

La Habana Vieja's largest cobbled square – the seat of the Spanish government – is the site of the city's first castle, the governor's mansion, El Templete and the natural history museum *(see p72)*.

8 Museo de la Revolución

This vast museum in the former Presidential Palace has a whole section dedicated to Che Guevara *(see p75)*.

La Habana Vieja, Havana

NEED TO KNOW

Palacio de los Capitanes Generales: **MAP X4**; Plaza de Armas; adm

Basílica Menor de San Francisco de Asís: **MAP X5**; Calle Oficios; adm CUP$6

Catedral de La Habana: **MAP X4**; Plaza de la Catedral, Empedrado

Calle Mercaderes: **MAP X5**

Museo Nacional de Bellas Artes: **MAP V4 & V5**; adm CUP$125

Plaza Vieja: **MAP X5**

Plaza de Armas: **MAP X4**; El Templete: open 9am–5pm Tue–Sat; adm

Museo de la Revolución: **MAP W4**; Calle Refugio & Agramonte; 7801 5598; open 10am–4:30pm daily; adm CUP$200

Calle Obispo: **MAP W5–X5**

Parque Histórico-Militar Morro-Cabaña: **MAP X1**; Habana del Este; adm CUP$200

The Modern City, Havana

Beyond La Habana Vieja, this lively, colorful metropolis of two million people radiates inland from the harbor and coastline like a Spanish fan, emerging from compact 19th-century *barrios* into more spacious 20th-century *municipios* and post-revolutionary suburbs. Apartment blocks give way to once-noble, upper-class districts full of Beaux Arts, Art Deco, and Modernist mansions, while concrete office blocks, government buildings, and hotels from the 1950s give a retro feel.

1 Universidad de La Habana

Havana University has a Neo-Colonial facade reached via a vast staircase. Its museums **(above)** showcase Cuba's flora, fauna, and pre-Columbian cultures.

2 Capitolio

A replica of Washington D.C.'s Capitol **(below)**, this restored Neo-Classical structure is once again the seat of the National Assembly. All points in Cuba are measured from a diamond inset in the floor.

3 Malecón

Stretching west from Paseo de Martí, the Malecón – Havana's seafront boulevard **(above)** – is the perfect place for a sunset stroll.

4 Avenida de los Presidentes

Flanked by mansions, this broad boulevard slopes north to the Malecón and is studded with monuments to deceased heroes and heads of state.

5 Paseo de Martí

Sloping from Parque Central to the Malecón, this tree-shaded boulevard – known colloquially by its former name of Prado – is a great place to meet locals. The area is full of school kids at play during the day.

6 Plaza de la Revolución

A vast, austere square surrounded by government buildings such as the Ministry of the Interior (left), this is the heart of state affairs, best visited during the May Day Parade when it is packed with people.

BIOTECH SUCCESS

One of the world's most advanced biotechnology and genetic engineering industries is concentrated in the western district of Siboney. The research facilities here are cutting edge, and treatments for illnesses such as cancer, AIDS, and meningitis as well as the COVID-19 vaccine, have been developed here.

7 Parque Central

This park (below) makes a good starting point from which to explore the city. With a statue of José Martí, regarded as Cuba's national hero, it is surrounded by hotels and several city attractions. Baseball fans often gather here for debates.

8 Hotel Nacional

A grandiose legacy of the 1930s, this landmark building is modeled on The Breakers, in Palm Beach, Florida. It has an international *Who's Who* list of past guests.

NEED TO KNOW

Universidad de La Habana: **MAP U2**; Calle L & San Lázaro; 7878 3231; open 9am–5pm Mon–Fri

Capitolio: **MAP V5**; Paseo de Martí & Calle Brasil; 7860 8454; open 10am–5pm Tue–Sun; CUP$250

Malecón: **MAP S1–W1**

Avenida de los Presidentes: **MAP T1–2**

Paseo de Martí: **MAP W1–2**

Plaza de la Revolución: **MAP T3**

Parque Central: **MAP V5**

Hotel Nacional: **MAP U1**; Calle O & Calle 21; 7836 3564

Cementerio Colón: **MAP S3–T3**; Av. Zapata & Calle 12, Vedado; 7881 5515; open 8am–5pm daily; adm CUP$125

9 Cementerio Colón

Havana's huge cemetery features an astonishing collection of elaborate tombs. Many of Cuba's most famous personalities are buried here.

10 Miramar

This region of western Havana, developed in the 20th century, features avenues lined with mansions and plush hotels set amid age-old fig trees.

The Modern City, Havana

TOP 10 ⭐ Cordillera de Guaniguanico

The pine-clad mountains that begin a short distance west of Havana and run through northern Pinar del Río province are a nature lover's paradise of protected national parks sheltering endangered fauna. The mountains grow more rugged westward, where tobacco plants thrive, dramatic rock formations called *mogotes* tower over lush valleys, and huge cavern systems attract cavers. Centered on a village that itself is a National Historic Monument, the Valle de Viñales is rural Cuba at its most sublime.

Parque Nacional de Viñales ①

This exquisite valley, the most scenic setting in Cuba, is remarkable for its limestone formations called *mogotes* **(right)**. Many of these massive structures are riddled with series of caves.

③ Las Terrazas

Built as a model rural community, this mountain village is a center for ecotourism and is known for its artists' studios and trails that lead to beautiful waterfalls and coffee farms.

④ Tobacco Farms

The valleys of Pinar del Río are renowned as centers for the production of the nation's finest cigar tobacco, often seen drying in sheds. The fields are tilled by ox-drawn ploughs even today.

⑤ Gran Caverna de Santo Tomás

Take a guided tour through Cuba's largest cave system – 28 miles (45 km) of galleries adorned with stalactites and stalagmites.

⑥ Rancho La Guabina

This lakeside horse-breeding center is set amid hills with trails **(below)**. Horseback riding is offered, and the farm can be explored in horse carriages. It has a lovely boutique hotel.

② Soroa

A lush retreat within the Sierra del Rosario Biosphere Reserve, Soroa **(above)** is famous for its hillside Orquideario – orchid garden – and scenic trails. Guests can enjoy treatments in a bath-house directly fed by the fresh mineral springs.

9 Cueva del Indio

Deep inside a *mogote*, this huge cavern lit by artificial lighting has fabulous dripstone formations. Having walked the floodlit trail, visitors can ride through an underground river **(left)** on a motorized boat.

MOGOTES

These round-topped rock formations are the remains of a limestone plateau. Water dissolved the rock over millions of years, creating chains of caverns. When the ceilings collapsed, they left these haystack mountains. Visit the Mural de la Prehistoria at Valle de Viñales, painted on a *mogote* by Leovigildo González Morillo.

10 Viñales

This small, pretty 19th-century village's **(above)** economy has always been based on agriculture. Oxcarts plod through quiet streets lined with traditional homes fronted by old-fashioned arcades.

7 Cueva de los Portales

Soaring to a lofty height of 100 ft (30 m), this cavern was Che Guevara's headquarters during the Cuban Missile Crisis. It has Che's old iron bed as well as giant stalagmites and stalactites.

8 Hiking

Las Terrazas, Soroa, and Viñales all have many official trails. A licensed guide – required for hiking into the mountains – can be hired at each of these starting points.

Cordillera de Guaniguanico

NEED TO KNOW

Parque Nacional de Viñales: **MAP B2**; 4879 6144

Soroa: **MAP C2**; 4852 3871; adm CUP$100, with guide

Las Terrazas: **MAP C2**; Autopista Habana-Pinar del Río, km 51; 4857 8700

Gran Caverna de San Tomás: **MAP B2**; Parque Nacional de Viñales; 4868 1214; open 9:30am–3:30pm daily; adm CUP$360

Rancho La Guabina: **MAP B3**; Carretera de Luís Lazo, km 9.5; 4875 7616; open 8am–5pm daily

Cueva de los Portales: **MAP C2**; Carretera San Andrés, km 14; open 8am–5pm daily

Cueva del Indio: **MAP B2**; Carretera Puerto Esperanza, km 36; 4879 6280; open 9am–4:45pm daily; adm CUP$120

TOP 10 ⭐ Zapata Peninsula

Protected within a huge biosphere reserve, the Zapata Peninsula is covered in swampland and forests teeming with wildlife. The coast is lined with sandy beaches and coral reef, attracting scuba divers. Many of the populace here once worked as *carboneros,* eking out a living making charcoal. The area is known for the Bahía de Cochinos (Bay of Pigs), site of the invasion *(see p37).*

Laguna del Tesoro ①

Accessed via a 3-mile (5-km) canal, "Treasure Lake" **(right)** is named for the gold that Taínos supposedly hid in its waters when Spanish *conquistadores* arrived. Regular boat tours visit a re-created Taíno village on an island that also hosts a resort hotel.

② Birding

Eighteen of Cuba's 28 endemic bird species *(see pp52–3)* inhabit Zapata, including *tocororo* and *zunzuncito* **(above)**. Flamingos tip-toe elegantly around Las Salinas lagoon, while sandhill cranes throng the reed beds.

③ Fishing

The saltwater shallows off southern Zapata teem with bonefish, while tarpon and *manjuarí* (alligator gar) inhabit the estuaries and tributaries of the Hatiguanico river.

Zapata Peninsula

④ Parque Nacional Ciénaga de Zapata

This vast wetland ecosystem can be explored on guided tours and boat trips. The mangroves, grasslands, and lagoons teem with wildlife.

⑤ Crocodile Farm

Visitors can photograph crocodiles **(left)** from an observation point overlooking the Boca de Guamá, which has Cuba's largest crocodile farm.

6 Museo Girón

Housing military hardware, including tanks and a Cuban air force plane **(above)**, this museum features items relating to the Bay of Pigs invasion and the three-day battle that followed.

7 Central Australia

Castro's headquarters during the Bay of Pigs invasion in 1961 was in the former administrative offices of the now-defunct Central Australia sugar mill. A steam train excursion operates from here into the countryside.

8 Caleta Buena

This splendid cove **(above)** with coral-filled turquoise waters is perfect for snorkeling and scuba diving. White sands top the coral shoreline.

9 Cenote de los Peces

With peacock-blue waters, this exquisite natural pool is 33 ft (10 m) deep, and has a side tunnel that descends 230 ft (70 m). Named for the fish that swim in it, this is a popular spot for cave-diving enthusiasts.

LA VICTORIA

Trained by the CIA, the anti-Castro exiles who landed at the Bay of Pigs on April 17, 1961 intended to link up with counter-revolutionaries in the rugged Sierra del Escambray. The site was ill chosen, as the landing craft grounded on reefs. The invasion was finally doomed when President John F. Kennedy refused to authorize the US naval and air support.

NEED TO KNOW

Laguna del Tesoro: **MAP F3**; 4591 5662; boats depart Boca 9am–3:30pm daily

Parque Nacional Ciénaga de Zapata: **MAP E3**; 4598 724; adm from CUP$360, extra with guide

Crocodile Farm: **MAP F3**; 4591 5666; open 8am–4pm daily; adm CUP$60

Caleta Buena: **MAP F3**; 4591 3224; open 9am– 5pm daily; adm

Cenote de los Peces: **MAP F3**; open 9am–4:30pm daily

Museo Girón: **MAP F3**; 4598 4122; open 9am–5pm daily; adm CUP$60; guide CUP$25

Central Australia: **MAP F3**; 4591 2504; open 8am–4:45pm Mon–Sat, 8am–noon Sun

10 Scuba Diving

Unspoiled coral reefs and a wall plunging 1,000 ft (305 m) lie close to the shore. Inland, *cenotes* – fresh water pit-caves – are suitable for experienced divers only.

TOP10 ★ Trinidad

Founded in 1514 by Diego Velázquez, Trinidad was made a UNESCO World Heritage Site in 1988. During the 17th and 18th centuries, the city grew rich from sugar production and the exploitation of slave labor. Sugar plantation owners and merchants built many of the city's homes and mansions. The cobblestone streets have barely changed since then; Trinidad feels like a town that time has passed by. Unlike most Cuban cities, Trinidad sits on a hill and is cooled by near-constant breezes.

Convento de San Francisco de Asís **1**

This ancient convent hosts a museum that recounts the fight against counter-revolutionaries *(see p37)*. The landmark bell tower **(right)** can be climbed for a commanding view of the historic center.

2 Plaza Mayor

This atmospheric, palm-shaded square **(above)** at the heart of the old city is surrounded by a cathedral and important mansions that today house museums and art galleries.

5 Nightlife

Trinidad is rightly celebrated for its after-dark ambience and, in particular, for traditional performances by Afro-Cuban troupes.

3 Shopping

Good bargains can be found at the crafts markets lining the streets, where locals sell hand-stitched lace and papier-mâché models of 1950s US automobiles.

6 Museo Romántico

The Palacio Brunet, now a museum, is furnished in period style. The beautiful architectural details include a carved cedar ceiling and *medio-puntos* – half-moon stained-glass windows.

Playa Ancón **4**

This is an immaculate beach **(right)** with turquoise waters on a peninsula 6 miles (10 km) from Trinidad. It is the setting for several hotels.

7 Casa de la Trova

Traditional music is played at the "House of the Troubador" **(left)**, on Plazuela de Segarte. This 1777 mansion is adorned with murals.

STEAM TRAINS

Until a decade ago, the country still had dozens of antique steam trains used for hauling sugarcane to the mills. A few have been restored and are now used for tours and excursions. Many have been refurbished as open-air museum pieces while the rest are no longer in use.

8 Valle de los Ingenios

This broad valley to the east of Trinidad is dotted with the atmospheric ruins of centuries-old sugar mills, including Hacienda Manaca Iznaga, which has a tower that can be climbed *(see p103)*.

Trinidad

NEED TO KNOW

Convento de San Francisco de Asís: **MAP Y1**; Calle Echerri 59; 4199 4121; open 9am–4pm Tue–Sun; adm CUP$50

Plaza Mayor: **MAP Z1**

Museo Romántico: **MAP Z1**; Calle Echerri & Calle Bolívar; 4199 4363; adm CUP$120; guide CUP$120

Casa de la Trova: **MAP Z1**; Calle Echerri 29; 4199 6445; open 10am–11pm daily

Museo Histórico: **MAP Y2**; Calle Bolívar 423; 4199 4460; open 9am–4pm Mon–Sat (to 1pm alternate Sun); adm CUP$120; guide CUP$70

■ Be wary of anyone claiming that your casa has closed – this may be a scam to stay at *casas particulares*.

9 La Boca

This rocky beach has spectacular views of the Escambray mountains (Sierra del Escambray). The sands are a great place to mingle with the locals.

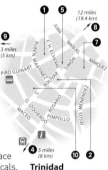

10 Museo Histórico

Housed in the Palacio Cantero **(above)**, the exhibits, including a fountain that once spouted *eau de cologne*, tell the town's story.

Following pages Street in central Havana

TOP 10 ⭐ Jardines del Rey

Rising from the Atlantic along the north shore of Ciego de Ávila and Camagüey provinces, this 280-mile- (450-km-) long archipelago, known as the King's Gardens, contains hundreds of islands. The major cays, Cayo Coco and Cayo Guillermo, are linked to the mainland by a *pedraplen* (causeway). Cayo Coco, Cayo Guillermo, and now Cayo Cruz all have tourist facilities. These tropical isles are popular with package vacationers. Flamingos wander the inshore lagoons, while other birds inhabit a nature preserve.

① Playa de los Flamencos

This lovely strip of white sand, stretching for 3 miles (5 km), is one of Cuba's most beautiful beaches. The crystal-clear turquoise waters are shallow enough for wading up to 650 ft (200 m) from the shore.

② Flamingos

Graceful flamingos **(above)** flock to the Laguna de los Flamencos from April to November. Parador La Silla is the best place to spot them flying overhead at sunrise and dusk.

③ Cayo Sabinal

This virginal island's beaches are fringed by a coral reef. Wild pigs inhabit the scrub-covered isle, and flamingos grace the inshore lagoons.

④ Cayo Guillermo

Connected to Cayo Coco by a raised highway, this island **(left)** is lined with beautiful, gently shelving beaches. Mangroves grow in the channel that separates the two islands. Dunes reach 59 ft (18 m) at Playa Pilar.

⑤ Watersports

Resort hotels offer a wide range of beach and ocean activities, including banana-boat rides and catamarans. Crystal-clear visibility reveals an exciting underwater world **(above)** for snorkelers and divers.

6 Cayo Cruz

Cayo Cruz, a long and narrow key, is reached by a *pedraplén*. It has three hotels on its sands, the smartest of which is the Iberostar Selection Esmeralda.

9 Cayo Coco

With miles of sandy beaches, Cayo Coco **(below)** is a haven for marine birds and a popular destination for families, divers, and watersports enthusiasts.

HEMINGWAY AND THE CAYS

During World War II, Ernest Hemingway patrolled off the north coast of Cuba in his sportfishing vessel, the *Pilar*. He outfitted his prized boat with hand grenades and machine guns and searched for Nazi submarines. His experiences in this region became the basis for his posthumously published novel *Islands in the Stream*.

10 Pedraplén

The highway linking Cayo Coco to the mainland runs ruler-straight across the Bahía de Perros, slicing it in two. At its north end, the road weaves through a series of small islands with herons, roseate spoonbills, and other wading birds.

7 Cayo Romano

Pristine Cayo Romano features one lodge, mostly used by anglers. Highlights include fly-fishing for bonefish, tarpon, and barracuda in the north shore lagoons.

Kiteboarding 8

Cayo Guillermo has optimal weather conditions for kitesurfing between October and May **(right)**. Havana Kiteboarding Club provides lessons.

NEED TO KNOW

Playa de los Flamencos: **MAP K2**

Cayo Sabinal: **MAP M3**

Cayo Guillermo: **MAP K2**

Cayo Coco: **MAP K2**

Pedraplén: **MAP K2**

Kiteboarding: **MAP K2**; www.havanakite boarding.com; adm

■ The cays were once reserved exclusively for tourists, but now Cubans can also access them. If arriving in a rental car, you will need to show your passport at the police checkpoints and tolls, where you could be searched for Cuban stowaways.

■ There are few places to eat outside the resort hotels. On Cayo Coco, three thatched beach grills (open 8am–8pm) at Playas de los Flamencos, Las Dunas, and Prohibida serve traditional Cuban dishes.

TOP 10 ⭐ Camagüey

A cradle of Cuban culture, the "City of Tinajones" lies in the heart of cattle country and was laid out with irregular streets designed as a convoluted maze to thwart pirates. The historic center is full of well-preserved colonial plazas and cobbled streets featuring antique churches and convents, as well as colorful 17th- and 18th-century domestic buildings with red-tile roofs, lathe-turned wooden window grills, and spacious interior courtyards adorned with the city's trademark oversized jars called *tinajones*.

Plaza San Juan de Dios **3**

A national monument, this plaza is lined with 18th-century pastel buildings **(right)** that reflect the local style. On the east side, a former church and military hospital houses a museum of colonial architecture.

1 Plaza del Carmen

Graced by a restored Baroque convent that has an art gallery, this cobblestone plaza is pedestrianized and features life-size ceramic figures of locals depicted in daily pursuits **(above)**.

4 Iglesia Sagrado Corazón de Jesús

This gracious, Neo-Gothic church dating from 1755 has been restored. It has a magnificent wooden ceiling, exquisite frescoes, and an elaborate gilt altar.

5 Iglesia Nuestra Señora de la Soledad

Built in 1776, this fine example of Cuban Baroque architecture has a lovely carved *alfarje* wood-paneled ceiling and painted pillars **(left)**. The famous local patriot, Ignacio Agramonte was baptized and married here.

6 Casa Natal Ignacio Agramonte

This former home of Ignacio Agramonte displays family furniture plus his personal belongings, including his pistol. It has an intimate courtyard with *tinajones*.

2 Catedral Nuestra Señora de la Merced

Dating from 1748, this Baroque church features noteworthy murals and the Santa Sepulcro, a figure of Christ atop a coffin cast from 23,000 silver coins.

Camagüey

7 Parque Agramonte

Dominated by a bronze equestrian statue of Ignacio Agramonte, the town's main square is surrounded by interesting colonial buildings, including the 18th-century cathedral with a six-story bell tower.

TINAJONES

Large earthenware jars up to 6 ft (2 m) wide called *tinajones* are a symbol of Camagüey. They were introduced by Catalonian immigrants in the early 1700s, and are used to collect rainwater, as well as for decorative purposes in courtyards and gardens.

NEED TO KNOW

MAP L3

Catedral Nuestra Señora de la Merced: Parque Agramonte

Iglesia Sagrado Corazón de Jesús: Parque Martí

Iglesia Nuestra Señora de la Soledad: Av. República and Agramonte

Casa Natal Ignacio Agramonte: Calle Agramonte 459; 3229 7116; open 9am–5:45pm Tue–Sat, 9am–noon Sun; adm CUP$5

Teatro Principal: Calle Padre Valencia; 3229 3048

Museo Ignacio Agramonte: Av. de los Mártires; 3228 2425; closed for renovation, call to check

■ Beware of hustlers trying to guide you to a *casa particular* (see p127).

8 Ballet de Camagüey

Second only to Havana's Ballet Nacional, Camagüey's renowned troupe **(below)** has toured over 40 countries. It was founded in 1967 by the prima ballerina Alicia Alonso (see p43).

9 Teatro Principal

This Neo-Classical theater (1850) was rebuilt in 1926. Its marble staircase is lit by a gilt chandelier. It is the principal venue for the acclaimed Ballet de Camagüey.

10 Museo Ignacio Agramonte

This eclectic museum housed in the former Spanish cavalry headquarters focuses on local and natural history and displays a collection of art.

TOP 10 ⭐ Holguín

This sprawling industrial city, known as the "City of Parks," radiates around a compact colonial core arranged in an easily navigated grid. Its many historic plazas include Parque Calixto García, named for the general who liberated the city from the Spanish in 1872. With its abundance of small museums, Holguín has an especially active cultural life. Some tourists bypass the town to visit the hilltop tourist complex of Mirador de Mayabe or the beach resort of Guardalavaca, which offers various ecological and archaeological attractions as well as spectacular scuba diving.

2 Plaza Calixto García

The most prominent feature of this large, tree-shaded plaza is the marble monument of General Calixto García **(left)**. The busy square is also home to the city's main museums. Casa Natal de Calixto García, where the general was born, is a block east of here.

5 Museo Provincial

The Neo-Classical building that houses this musem used to be a social club for the Spanish elite. Displays include historical artifacts, most notably the Hacha de Holguín – a pre-Columbian green peridot axe carved with human motifs.

3 Plaza San José

This cobbled square is the most intimate of the city's plazas and a pleasant place to sit on a bench beneath shady trees. Surrounded by colonial buildings, it is home to the Iglesia de San José, which is topped by a domed clocktower **(below)**.

1 Mirador de Mayabe

Offering a stunning vista over the Mayabe valley, full of beautiful towering royal palms, this lookout is the setting for a hotel, a country-style restaurant, and a cliff-top pool with a bar.

Holguín

- 8 — 18 miles (29 km)
- 10 — 1 mile (1.6 km)
- 3 — 31 miles (49 km)
- 7 — 34 miles (54 km)
- 1 — 6 miles (9.5 km)

CALLE AGRAMONTE
C. MARTINEZ
CALLE ARIAS
CALLE MACEO
CALLE AGUILERA
CALLE FREXES
CALLE MIRO
CALLE MANDULEY
CALLE MARTI
C. M. GOMEZ
MORALES
C. LUZ. CABALLERO

4 Plaza de la Marqueta

A ruined former market has been restored at the heart of this plaza, which features life-sized bronze figures. It is lined with shops including the Cuban Book Institute's Linotype print shop.

6 Casa de la Trova

This is one of Cuba's liveliest music venues with two programs daily. It is named for Faustino Oramas "El Guayabero" Osorio, who played the guitar here until his death in 2007, at the age of 96.

ORGANS

The Fábrica de Órganos at Carretera de Gibara 301 is the only Cuban factory still making mechanical hand-operated *órganos pneumáticos* (air-compression organs) using the traditional methods. They are fed with cards punched with the score. There is no guarantee that you will see or hear one being played.

NEED TO KNOW

Mirador de Mayabe: **MAP N4**; Alturas de Mayabe; 2442 2160; open 9am–7pm daily

Casa Natal de Calixto García: **MAP N4**; Frexes & Miró; 2442 5610; open 9am–4:30pm Tue–Sat; adm CUP$1

Museo Provincial: **MAP N4**; Calle Frexes 198; 2446 3395; open 8am–4:30pm Tue–Sat, 8am–noon Sun; adm

Playa Guardalavaca: **MAP P4**

Chorro de Maíta: **MAP N4**; Carretera Guardalavaca-Banes; 2443 0201; open 9am–5pm Mon–Sat (to 1pm Sun)

■ Holguín bustles with events during Semana de la Cultura Holguinera in January.

7 Playa Guardalavaca

A one-hour drive northeast of Holguín, this resort is lined with wonderful beaches and unspoiled coral reefs **(above)** that tempt diving enthusiasts.

8 Gibara

A windswept coastal town, Gibara was once a prominent port protected by a fortress. Known as "Villa Blanca" (White City), it is packed with colonial buildings. It also has several museums, and is home to an annual festival of cinema.

9 Chorro de Maíta

Cuba's largest Indigenous burial site **(below)**, Chorro de Maíta is an archaeological treasure with skeletons and funerary offerings on display. Adjacent to it is a re-created Taíno village called Aldea Taína.

10 Loma de la Cruz

With views over the town, this hill is named for the Holy Cross at its summit and can be reached via 485 steps. It is the site for the Romerias de Mayo pilgrimage every May.

🔟 ⭐ Santiago de Cuba

The country's second-oldest and second-largest city has a flavor all its own as the most African, and the most musical city, in Cuba. It was founded in 1515 on the hilly east shore of a deep, flask-shaped bay. Its colonial core is full of historic buildings, while its fascinating past as the second capital of Cuba is enriched by its importance as a hotbed of political upheaval. Fidel Castro studied here and later initiated the Revolution with an attack on the Moncada barracks. Santiago explodes with colorful frenzy during Carnaval each July.

Panoramic view of Santiago de Cuba

1 El Morro
At the entrance to Santiago Bay, the 17th-century El Morro castle **(above)** offers stunning coastal vistas. Soldiers in period costume march onto the ramparts and fire a cannon at dusk.

2 Museo Emilio Bacardí
Visitors can view colonial-era armaments, relics from the slave trade, and a superlative body of paintings and sculptures in Cuba's oldest museum **(above)**.

3 Plaza de la Revolución
This vast plaza was used primarily for political rallies and features a massive monument of General Antonio Maceo.

4 Reserva de la Biosfera Baconao
Just east of Santiago, this reserve features a classic car museum, artist communities, on a mountain coffee estate, and a lovely tropical garden *(see p114)*.

5 Parque Céspedes
At the heart of the city, this square is lined with historic buildings such as the Museo Ambiente Histórico and the Catedral de la Asunción.

NEED TO KNOW

MAP P6

El Morro: Carretera al Morro, km 7.5; 2269 1569; open 9am–4pm Mon–Sat, 9am–1pm Sun; adm CUP$100

Museo Emilio Bacardí: Calle Pío Rosado; 2265 4501; open 1–5pm Mon–Sat, 9am–2pm Sun; adm CUP$6

Cementerio Santa Ifigenia: Avenida Capitán Raúl Perozo; 2263 1626; open 8am–4pm daily; adm CUP$75

Cuartel Moncada: Avenida Moncada; 2266 1157; open 9am–4:30pm Tue–Sat, 9am–12:30pm Sun & Mon; adm

6 Vista Alegre

A residential district, Vista Alegre features mansions and Modernist homes. The Casa del Caribe and Museo de las Religiones Populares honor the city's rich Afro-Cuban culture.

8 Cementerio Santa Ifigenia

Many important figures are buried here, including Fidel Castro, interred in 2016 adjacent to José Martí (see p37), whose guard of honor changes every half hour.

VIRGEN DE LA CARIDAD DEL COBRE

Miraculous powers are ascribed to the Virgin of Charity, Cuba's patron saint, who is personified as a Black Madonna holding a Black Christ. According to Cuban legend, three fishermen were caught in a storm in 1608 and survived because a statue of the Virgin appeared in the bay, calming the rough seas for them.

Santiago de Cuba

7 El Cobre

This village is famous for the Basílica de Nuestra Señora de la Caridad del Cobre (below), Cuba's most important church, where pilgrims gather to pray to the Virgin of Charity.

9 Cuartel Moncada

The setting for Castro's attack on July 26, 1953 (see p37), this former military barracks (above) is today a school housing the Museo Histórico 26 de Julio recalling the failed venture, as well as exhibits recounting a general history of Cuba.

10 Plaza Dolores

Popular, tree-shaded Plaza Dolores is a pleasant place to relax. The former Iglesia de Nuestra Señora de los Dolores church on the east side now functions as a venue for classical concerts.

🔟⭐ Baracoa

Tucked inside a broad bay enfolded by mountains, Baracoa sits at the far northeast corner of Cuba. It was founded in 1511 as the island's first settlement and capital. When governor Velázquez moved to Santiago, a long period of isolation set in. Locals claim that the Bahía de Miel was the site of Columbus' first landing in Cuba in 1492, and that the flat-topped mountain he described is El Yunque, which rises behind Baracoa. Lined with wooden houses in local style, the town now buzzes with tourists, and is particularly popular with independent travelers.

Plaza Independencia ③

This small plaza **(right)** has a bust of the Taíno chief Hatüey in front of the Catedral de Nuestra Señora de la Asunción, where you can see a wooden cross said to have been brought to Cuba by Columbus.

① Fuerte Matachín

Guarding the eastern entrance to town, this tiny fortress contains a museum that traces the history of Baracoa and a collection of polymitas – colored snails **(above)** particular to the region.

② Bahía de Baracoa

This flask-shaped bay **(below)** to the west of town is lined by a gray-sand beach, backed by thickly forested Alturas de Baracoa mountains.

④ Museo Arqueológico

Full of fascinating drip-stone formations, the Cueva de Paraíso hosts an archaeological museum with Taíno artifacts and a funerary cave displaying skeletons.

⑤ Hotel El Castillo

Built to repel the British, the Castillo de Seboruco fortress now houses a hotel *(see p129)* with sensational views of the El Yunque mountain and Baracoa.

⑥ Regional Cuisine

Baracoa is known for its cuisine based on creative uses of coconut, such as the *cucurucho*, a coconut dessert mixed with fruits and honey.

Baracoa

Atlantic Ocean

AVE DE LOS MARTIRES
MALECÓN
ANTONIO MACEO
JOSÉ MARTÍ
CALIXTO GARCÍA
FLOR
MALECÓN
CROMBET
RODNEY
CÉSPEDES
CALIXTO GARCÍA
ABEZ
DÍAZ
MONCADA
JOSÉ MARTÍ

⑦ 6 miles (9.5 km)
⑩ 4 miles (6.4 km)

25 miles (40 km) ⑧

8 Punta Maisí
Accessed via a coastal highway, this most easterly point of the island of Cuba is marked by a lighthouse **(left)**, built in 1862. On a clear day, it is possible to see Haiti from here.

POLYMITAS

The polymita genus of snail, endemic to the Baracoa region, is known for its multi-colored shell with a whorled pattern. Each snail has a unique pattern and color. With a dwindling population, the polymita is now endangered. You are advised not to buy any shells or shell necklaces offered for sale.

NEED TO KNOW

MAP R5

Fuerte Matachín: Calle Martí; 2164 2122; open 8am–noon, 2–6pm Mon–Sat, 8am–noon Sun; adm

Catedral de Nuestra Señora de la Asunción: Plaza Independencia; 2164 2595; open 7:30–11am & 4–9pm Tue–Sun

Museo Arqueológico: 9am–5pm daily; adm

■ If you are curious about Baracoa's cocoa heritage, head to Finca de las Mujeres *(Carretera Baracoa-Yumurí, El Güirito)* and learn about Cuban cacao and local sweets.

■ The colorful El Poeta is a great place to try local food, served in a unique style *(see p117)*.

7 El Yunque
An anvil-shaped mountain formation **(above)**, El Yunque rises above lush rainforests that provide an ideal habitat for rare species of flora and fauna.

9 Hiking
Guided hikes into the rainforests to the south of town lead into the mountains. Birders still hope to spot the ivory-billed woodpecker, threatened by extinction.

10 Playa Duaba
This black-sand beach west of Baracoa features a monument to General Antonio Maceo, who landed here in 1895 and fought the first battle of the War of Independence.

The Top 10
of Everything

Valle de Viñales

🔟 Moments in History

1 **c.500 BC: Taíno Culture**
The Taíno people arrived from the Orinoco region of South America on the island they called Cuba. Worshipping gods of nature, this peaceful society was organized into villages led by *caciques* (chieftains).

2 **1492: Columbus Arrives**
The Genoese explorer sighted Cuba during his first voyage and renamed it Juana. In 1509, Columbus' son Diego conquered the island and decimated the Taínos. *Conquistador* Diego Velázquez founded the first town, Baracoa, in 1511.

3 **1762: The English Occupy Cuba**
The height of the Spanish colony ended when English troops seized Havana. England opened Cuba to free trade and expanded the slave trade. In 1763, Havana was returned to Spain in exchange for Florida.

4 **1868: Ten Years' War**
Landowner Carlos Manuel de Céspedes freed his enslaved people and revolted against Spanish rule. A guerrilla war ensued, in which towns were razed and the economy devastated. Later, US companies bought up Cuban sugar plantations.

Second War of Independence (1895–98)

5 **1895: Second War of Independence**
Exiled nationalist José Martí returned to lead the fight for independence. Though martyred in battle, his forces gained the upper hand, but were sidelined after the USS *Maine* was destroyed in Havana harbor. The US declared war on Spain, and invaded Cuba, occupying it.

6 **1902: Independence**
Following four years of US military rule, Washington granted the island its independence. A period of mostly corrupt government followed, while US corporations came to dominate the Cuban sugar-based economy. In 1906, following a revolt against president Palma, the US re-occupied the island for four years.

A sugarcane plantation in Havana

7 1953–59: Castro Triumphs

Castro launched the Cuban Revolution with an audacious attack that failed. On New Year's Eve 1958, General Fulgencio Batista fled Cuba, and Castro delivered a victory speech. A newly formed democratic government was quickly usurped by Castro, who later allied with the Soviet Union and initiated dramatic reforms.

Fidel Castro enters Havana

8 1961: Bay of Pigs Invasion

CIA-trained Cuban exiles stormed ashore to assist Cuban-based counter-revolutionaries in toppling Castro. The attack was repelled, and Castro took advantage of popular sentiment against the US-inspired invasion to announce that Cuba would be socialist.

9 1991: Período Especial Begins

Thirty years of economic support ended overnight when the Soviet Union collapsed. The economy imploded, and Cubans faced extreme hardship, triggering a mass exodus to the US on flimsy rafts. Since 1994, the crisis has eased with a tourism boom helping to promote recovery.

10 2011–Present: Cuban Thaw

In 2011, US President Barack Obama lifted restrictions against Americans visiting Cuba, and renewed diplomatic relations with the country in 2015. The thaw didn't last long, however; in 2017, President Donald Trump reinstated many travel restrictions on Cuba.

TOP 10 CUBA FIGURES

1 Christopher Columbus (1451–1506)
Genoese explorer and the first European to sight Cuba on October 28, 1492.

2 Hatüey (died 1512)
Heroic Taíno chieftain who led resistance to Spanish colonial rule and was burned at the stake.

3 Carlos Manuel de Céspedes (1819–74)
The "Father of the Homeland" freed enslaved people and launched the wars for independence.

4 José Martí (1853–95)
Cuba's foremost celebrated writer and leader martyred in battle.

5 Máximo Gómez (1836–1905)
Dominican-born general and supreme commander of the Cuban liberation army.

6 Antonio Maceo Grajales (1845–96)
Guerrilla leader in the independence wars, Grajales was killed in battle.

7 Calixto García (1839–98)
Second-in-command of the independence army, and liberator of many Spanish-held cities.

8 Gerardo Machado (1871–1939)
Corrupt dictator who ruled Cuba with an iron fist between 1924 and 1933, when he was forced into exile.

9 Fulgencio Batista (1901–73)
General who seized power in 1934 and ruled Cuba until he fled on New Year's Eve in 1958.

10 Fidel Castro (1926–2016)
Former head of state who led the Revolution. Castro held power for five decades.

Calixto García

🔟 Revolution Sites

Salon de los Espejos (Hall of Mirrors) at the Museo de la Revolución

1 Museo de la Revolución

The independence struggle, the effort to topple Batista, and the subsequent building of socialism are highlighted in this museum *(see p13)*. It is housed in the former presidential palace, which was built in 1920 and fitted with lavish interior decoration. The caricatures in the "Corner of Cretins" poke fun at Batista and at US presidents Reagan, and Bush Sr and Jr.

2 Presidio Modelo

This model prison, completed in 1936, accommodated Fidel and Raúl Castro as well as 25 other revolutionaries sentenced to imprisonment following the Moncada attack. The hospital wing where they slept is now a museum *(see p87)*, while Fidel's private room with its marble bathroom contains a collection of the books he read during his years of incarceration.

3 Granma Memorial

MAP V4 ■ Calle Colón, Havana ■ 7862 4091 ■ Open 9am–5pm daily ■ Adm

The *Granma*, the vessel in which Castro sailed to Cuba with his guerrilla army, is displayed within a glass case in an open-air plaza to the rear of the Museo de la Revolución. Exhibits at the memorial include military hardware left over from the Bay of Pigs invasion.

4 Mausoleo y Museo del Segundo Frente

MAP P5 ■ Av. de los Mártires, Mayarí Arriba ■ 2242 5749 ■ Open 9am–4:30pm Mon–Sat, 9am–noon Sun

The small town of Mayarí Arriba commemorates combatants of the Second Front, led by Raúl Castro. The complex includes a museum exhibiting armaments and warplanes, and a landscaped mausoleum, framed by royal palms, includes the future grave of Raúl.

Presidio Modelo

5 La Comandancia de la Plata

MAP M6 ■ Parque Nacional Pico Turquino, 5 miles (8 km) from Villa Santo Domingo ■ EcoTur, Bayamo; 2348 7006; departures from 8:15am ■ Adm

A permit and guide are required to visit Castro's former guerrilla headquarters. Visits can be booked at the Ecotur office in Hotel Sierra Maestra.

6 Cuartel Moncada

Bullet holes riddle the walls of this former military barracks that sustained attacks by Castro's rebels on July 26, 1953, in the opening salvo to topple Batista. The building is now a school and includes the Museo Histórico 26 de Julio *(see p31)*, full of gory mementos.

7 Monumento del Che

A massive bronze figure of Che Guevara stands over bas-reliefs of Che in combat. Beneath and to the rear, the Museo del Che is Cuba's principal museum dedicated to the Argentinian revolutionary, whose remains are interred in an adjacent mausoleum *(see p97)*.

8 Complejo Histórico Abel Santamaría

MAP P6 ■ Av. de los Libertadores, Santiago de Cuba ■ 2262 4119 ■ Open 9am–5pm Mon–Sat ■ Adm

A Modernist cube with a bas-relief of revolutionary Abel Santamaría

Complejo Histórico Abel Santamaría

overlooks this park, where his rebel corps fired on Moncada. A museum honoring Santamaría is housed in the colonial former Civil Hospital Saturnino Lora building, later used for the trial of Fidel Castro.

9 Museo de la Lucha Clandestina

MAP P6 ■ Calle Rabí 1, Santiago de Cuba ■ 2262 4689 ■ Open 9am–4:45pm daily ■ Adm

This museum in the former headquarters of Batista's police force tells the story of the brave M-26-7 revolutionaries in Santiago who assaulted the building in November 1956.

10 Granjita Siboney

MAP P6 ■ Carretera a Siboney, km 13.5 ■ 2239 9168 ■ Open 9am–1pm Mon, 9am–4:30pm Tue–Sun ■ Adm

Castro launched the attack on Moncada from this farmhouse *(see p40)*, which is now a museum. Batista's forces then attacked it and dumped the rebel bodies here.

Monumento del Che

HASTA LA VICTORIA SIEMPRE

TOP 10 Moments in Fidel Castro's Life

1 Birth and Childhood

Born on August 13, 1926, to a rural patriarch and his maid at Birán in Holguín province, Fidel Castro was raised by his mother and was not formally recognized by his father until he turned 17.

Fidel Castro as a child

2 Jesuit Schooling

Castro was educated by Jesuits in Santiago de Cuba, and later at Belén College in Havana. Although combative, he excelled in his studies and was named Cuba's top student athlete.

3 University

Castro entered the University of Havana law school in 1945, where he became embroiled in politics as a student leader, and graduated in 1950. He made national headlines several times as an outspoken critic of the government.

4 Attack on Moncada

After Batista overthrew the constitutional government and cancelled elections in March 1953, Castro initiated a legal petition against him. It failed, and he launched his revolution with an assault on the Moncada Barracks on July 26, 1953.

Moncada Barracks, with bullet holes

5 Prison

After giving his impassioned "History Will Absolve Me" speech in 1953, Castro was sent to prison for 15 years. He used the time to organize his forces. Amnestied in May 1955, he set up a guerrilla army during exile in Mexico.

6 War in the Sierra Maestra

After his exile ended, Castro initiated a plan to return to Cuba. On landing in the Granma province in 1956, his forces were ambushed, but Castro, Raúl Castro, and Che Guevara escaped and established their headquarters (see p39). Castro directed the opposition from here, winning several battles and slowly taking control of Cuba.

Castro giving rifle training to new recruits in his revolutionary army

7 Batista Toppled

Castro pledged to support a provisional democratic government after his forces ousted Batista in 1959. Meanwhile, separate guerrilla columns, led by Che Guevara and Camilo Cienfuegos, won key victories. When Santa Clara fell to Che Guevara's troops on New Year's Eve, 1958, Batista fled the country, and Castro triumphantly returned to Havana.

8 Bay of Pigs

A democratic government was founded, but Castro usurped it and initiated dramatic socialist reforms. This resulted in a massive exodus of Cubans. A group of unhappy exiles, trained by the CIA, landed at the Bay of Pigs on April 17, 1961 to invade Cuba, but were quickly defeated.

9 Cuban Missile Crisis

In December 1961, Castro declared Cuba a Marxist-Leninist state. He signed a pact with the Soviet Union, which installed nuclear missiles in Cuba in 1962. However, the US President Kennedy demanded their withdrawal. The nations stood on the brink of nuclear war until Soviet President Khrushchev backed down.

Soviet freighter Anosov, thought to have been carrying missiles to Cuba

10 Castro Dies

In August 2006, Fidel Castro underwent surgery for acute diverticulitis from which he never fully recovered. He eventually resigned and Raúl Castro was elected president on 24 February, 2008. Fidel died on November 25, 2016 and was buried in Santiago de Cuba.

TOP 10 REVOLUTION FIGURES

Che Guevara

1 Che Guevara (1928–67)
Doctor-turned-revolutionary who became Minister of Finance & Industry and steered Cuba into socialism.

2 Raúl Castro (1931–)
The younger brother of Fidel, a lifelong communist and Cuban president from 2006 to 2018.

3 Camilo Cienfuegos (1932–59)
Chief of Staff in Fidel's guerrilla army. He went missing on a night flight in October 1959, and neither his plane nor he have ever been found.

4 José Antonio Echeverría (1932–57)
Student leader who gave a dramatic "Three Minutes of Truth" speech on Cuban national radio before being shot dead by a police patrol.

5 Julio Antonio Mella (1903–29)
The founder of the Cuban Communist Party; he was murdered in Mexico.

6 Jesús Menéndez (1911–48)
Socialist labor agitator who worked on behalf of local sugarcane workers.

7 Frank País (1934–57)
A principal leader in the M-26-7 movement, País was murdered by Batista's police.

8 Abel Santamaría (1927–53)
Castro's probable successor, Abel Santamaría was murdered while a prisoner after the Moncada attack.

9 Haydée Santamaría (1923–80)
Abel's sister was captured at Moncada, but managed to survive the torture.

10 Celia Sánchez (1920–80)
Middle-class socialist who ran the supply line for Castro's guerrilla army and later became his secretary.

🔟 Writers and Artists

Cuban writer Alejo Carpentier

① Alejo Carpentier (1904–80)

Carpentier is known for his cultural journalism focused on Afro-Cuban traditions. He was sent into exile for opposing General Machado. After the Revolution (see p37), he headed Cuba's state publishing house.

② Amelia Peláez (1896–1968)

Influenced by Matisse and Picasso, this ceramicist and painter is best known for her vast mural of blue, black, and white glass tiles adorning Hotel Habana Libre (see p77).

③ José Martí (1853–95)

Perhaps the leading Latin American essayist, poet, and journalist of the 19th century, Martí led the Independence movement (see p36). He wrote profusely for the cause of social justice, pan-Americanism, and liberty.

④ Wifredo Lam (1902–82)

Born in Sagua la Grande, Lam befriended many leading European painters while living in Paris. His works reflect Afro-Cuban culture.

⑤ Dulce María Loynaz (1902–97)

The doyenne of Cuban poetry, Loynaz went into relative seclusion following the Revolution, after her husband fled Cuba. Her works were rediscovered in the 1980s. An erotic intensity infuses many of her works.

⑥ Nicolás Guillén (1902–89)

Considered the poet laureate of Cuba, Guillén's African heritage is reflected in his distinctive *poesía negra* (Black poetry). He joined the Communist Party at an early age and became president of the National Union of Writers and Artists.

⑦ René Portocarrero (1912–85)

One of Cuba's master painters and sculptors, Portocarrero is well represented in the Museo Nacional

The Jose Martí Monument in Parque Central Havana

René Portocarrero's *Diablito* (1966)

de Bellas Artes *(see p12)*, and his murals are also in the Teatro Nacional and Hotel Habana Libre. His work is infused with religious icons.

⑧ Guillermo Cabrera Infante (1929–2005)

This critic, journalist, and novelist is best known for *Tres Tristes Tigres*, his seminal novel about the sordid era of pre-revolutionary Havana. Post-Revolution, he edited a key literary magazine before being exiled for criticizing Castro's government.

⑨ José Lezama Lima (1910–76)

Known as much for his personal life as for his Baroque writing, Lima was persecuted following the Revolution for presiding over the jury that awarded "dissident" writer Herberto Padilla a prize for his book. His most famous work is the semi-biographical *Paradiso*.

⑩ Manuel Mendive (b.1944)

Mendive is considered to be Cuba's most visionary and influential living artist. His works are both naive and highly erotic. A practising *santero (see pp48–9)*, Mendive is represented in museums around the world.

TOP 10 OTHER FAMOUS CUBANS

1 Carlos Finlay (1833–1915)
The doctor who discovered that yellow fever is transmitted by mosquitoes.

2 José Raúl Capablanca (1888–1942)
The "Mozart of chess," as he was known, held the World Chess Championship title from 1921 to 1927.

3 Celia Cruz (1925–2003)
Known as the "Queen of Salsa", she wowed audiences with her style and multiple records.

4 Alberto Díaz Gutiérrez (1928–2001)
This photographer, better known as Alberto Korda, shot the iconic image of Che Guevara.

5 Tomás Gutiérrez Alea (1928–96)
A brilliant film-maker, "Titón" was at the forefront of New Latin American cinema in the 1960s and 70s.

6 Eligio Sardiñas (1910–88)
Called "Kid Chocolate" by his fans, this boxing prodigy was also a party man.

7 Alicia Alonso (1920–2019)
Cuba's *prima ballerina assoluta* who founded the National Ballet of Cuba.

8 Teófilo Stevenson (1952–2012)
Considered one of the greatest boxers of all time, this Olympic gold medal winner refused to turn professional.

9 Ana Fidelia Quirot (b.1963)
A track and field athlete who survived severe burns to win a silver medal at the 1996 Olympics.

10 Javier Sotomayor (b.1967)
Incredible high jumper, with an 8-ft (2.45-m) jump in 1993. He is still the world record holder for the sport.

Alicia Alonso and Igor Youskevitch

📟 American Legacies

Classic American cars in vibrant colors on a Cuban street

① American Autos

Time seems to have stood still for six decades on Cuban roads, where one in every five cars dates back to before the Revolution *(see p37)*. Most are American classics from the 1950s – including many iconic models that vanished from US roads years ago.

② Art Deco

Cuban cities are graced with Art Deco buildings that date back to the 1930s and the heyday of Hollywood movies. The finest are the cinemas, often with rounded architectural elements and horizontal banding. These designs exemplify the architects' desire to imbue local buildings with slick, streamlined forms, reflecting the great age of transport.

③ Harley-Davidsons

Many pre-revolutionary Harleys still roar around the streets of Cuba, maintained by passionate *harlistas* who are dedicated to keeping their "hogs" on the road by whatever means.

Industriales baseball team

④ Baseball

Americans visitors introduced baseball to Cuba in the mid-19th century. Today, the island produces some excellent players. Cuban teams regularly defeat US teams at the Olympic Games.

⑤ US Naval Base
MAP Q6

When the US government wrote Cuba's Constitution in 1902 *(see p36)*, it included a clause called the Platt Amendment, which granted itself a perpetual lease on Guantánamo Bay. Despite thawing relations between the US and Cuba, the naval base remains a bone of contention. The US government writes a check every year for the annual lease, but the government *(see pp40–41)* refuses to cash it.

Art Deco Bacardi Building, Havana

6 **Hotel Nacional**
Symbolic of Havana's decadent pre-revolutionary heyday, this hotel was built in 1930 in Spanish Neo-Classical style and was closely associated with the Mafia. The bar doubles as a museum to the many international VIPs who have stayed here (see p15).

7 **Malecón**
Havana's seafront boulevard was laid out in 1902 by US Army General Leonard Woods. Now officially known as Avenida Antonio Maceo, it is lined with late 19th-century buildings and high-rise hotels (see p14).

8 **Hotel Habana Libre**
This national monument opened in March 1958 as the Havana Hilton. Built in Modernist style with 630 rooms, it was the largest and tallest hotel in Latin America. The hotel also once served as Fidel Castro's headquarters (see p77).

9 **Ernest Hemingway**
The famous US author first came to Cuba in 1932 to fish for marlin. He fell in love with the island, and in 1939 bought Finca Vigía (see p47) outside Havana. His home for 20 years, the finca was where most of his novels were written.

10 **Steam Trains**
Creaking engines and carriages piled with sugarcane were once a common sight in Cuba. Now retired, dozens of these trains are on display in museums throughout the island. Most were made in Philadelphia in the 1920s.

Cuban steam train

TOP 10 AMERICAN AUTOS

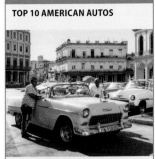

Sleek 1955 Chevrolet Bel-Air

1 1955 Chevrolet Bel-Air
This perfectly proportioned 1950s icon is ubiquitous in Cuba.

2 1958 Edsel Corsair
Launched in 1958, the Edsel Corsair's styling drew more laughs than praise. Production of the flamboyant folly ended the following year.

3 1959 Cadillac Eldorado
Reflecting the pinnacle of exorbitant late-1950s styling, this rocket-like car was inspired by the space race.

4 1951 Chevrolet Styline
This Chevy was the most commonly seen classic car in Cuba.

5 1950 Studebaker Champion
Its unmistakable bullet-nose design proved to be popular with Cubans.

6 1951 Kaiser Traveler
Ahead of its time, this excellent car had many safety features that the US government would later mandate.

7 1951 Pontiac Chieftain
This car had a likeness of a Native American chieftain on its hood, which lit up when the headlights were on.

8 1953 Buick Super
Famed for its "grinning tooth" grill, this car had a Dynaflow three-speed transmission nicknamed "Dynaslush" on account of its slow responsiveness.

9 1951 Hudson Hornet
Its ground-hugging profile and power made it a winner in stock-car racing.

10 1952 Oldsmobile Super 88
This behemoth had power steering and a lightweight body that promised effortless "one finger" parking.

🔟 Museums

Museo Nacional de Bellas Artes

1 Museo Nacional de Bellas Artes

This fine arts museum is home to Ancient Egyptian, Greek, and Roman art, and the works of European Old Masters. The Cuban section demonstrates the vitality and range of homegrown art, from the colonial period to the contemporary era *(see p12)*.

2 Museo de Artes Decorativas

MAP T1–T2 ■ Calle 17 502, Vedado, Havana ■ 7832 0924 ■ Open 9:30am–4pm Tue–Sat ■ Adm

Lavish furnishings fill this former Beaux Arts residence of a Cuban countess and reveal the tastes of the 19th-century ruling classes – from the French Rococo furniture and 17th-century Italian sculptures to the pink marble Art Deco bathroom.

3 Museo de Arquitectura Colonial

MAP H4 ■ Plaza Mayor, Trinidad ■ 4199 3208 ■ Open 9am–4pm Mon, Tue, Thu–Sat & alternate Sun ■ Adm

The former mansion of the Sánchez-Iznaga family is today dedicated to colonial architecture, with excellent displays that trace the evolution of Trinidad's unique style, from the town's founding to the 20th century.

4 Museo Oscar María de Rojas

MAP F2 ■ Calzada between Vives and Jénez, Cárdenas ■ 4552 2417 ■ Open 9am–4:45pm Tue–Sat, 9am–1:45pm Sun ■ Adm

Each of this museum's 14 salons has its own theme, from pre-Columbian culture to the Wars of Independence. Highlights include the coin room, the fascinating Baroque 19th-century hearse, and the beautifully restored former governor's mansion that houses the museum.

Museo Napoleónico

5 Museo Napoleónico

MAP U2 ■ Calle San Miguel 412, Vedado, Havana ■ 7879 1460 ■ Open 9:30am–2pm Tue–Fri ■ Adm

This museum, set in a 1920s palazzo, is replete with paintings, sculptures, and mementos of the life and death of Napoleon Bonaparte.

6 Museo de la Ciudad

MAP X4 ■ Calle Tacón, Plaza de Armas, Havana ■ 7866 8183 ■ Open 9:30am–5pm Tue–Sun ■ Adm

The museum in the Palacio de los Capitanes Generales exhibits flags, colonial-era armaments, and a throne room built for the king of Spain, who never actually visited.

Museo de la Ciudad

7 Museo del Ron Havana Club

MAP X5 ▪ Fundación Destilería Havana Club, Avenida del Puerto 262, La Habana Vieja, Havana ▪ 7861 8051 ▪ Open 9am–5:30pm Mon–Fri

This museum explores the history and distillation of Cuba's famous rum. Exhibits include a large-scale model of a sugar mill.

8 Museo Ernest Hemingway

Finca Vigía, Ernest Hemingway's former home, where he lived for 20 years, has been left untouched since his departure from Cuba in 1960. It still contains his books and hunting trophies. His sportfishing vessel, *Pilar*, sits beneath a pavilion in the garden *(see p76)*.

Museo Ernest Hemingway

9 Museo Emilio Bacardí

Cuba's oldest museum is housed in a Neo-Classical mansion. It houses relics dating from the Spanish conquest to the wars of independence, as well as a collection related to slavery. Important Cuban art is found upstairs and includes works by Wifredo Lam *(see p30)*.

10 Museo de la Guerra Hispano-Cubano-Norteamericano

MAP P6 ▪ Carretera a Siboney, km 13.5 ▪ 2239 9119 ▪ Open 9am–5pm Mon–Sat ▪ Adm

Situated outside the coastal hamlet of Siboney, this museum recalls the 1898 Spanish-American War, with many battle sites located nearby. Exhibits include artillery, torpedoes, uniforms, photographs, and bas-relief maps.

TOP 10 CASTLES

Stately Castillo de la Real Fuerza

1 Castillo de la Real Fuerza (1577)
MAP X4
Havana's oldest fortress has angular ramparts surrounded by a broad moat.

2 El Morro (1589–1610)
MAP X1
This 16th-century castle stands at the entrance to Havana harbor.

3 Castillo de San Salvador de la Punta (1590–1630)
MAP W1
Opposite Havana's El Morro, the two were once linked by a heavy chain.

4 El Morro (1638)
MAP P6
El Morro offers dramatic views at the entrance to Santiago Bay.

5 Castillo de San Severino (1680–1745)
MAP E2
This 18th-century castle protected the Matanzas harbor channel.

6 Castillo Seburuco (1741)
MAP R5
Baracoa's hilltop castle is now a hotel.

7 Castillo de Jagua (1745)
MAP G3
Guarding Cienfuegos bay, this castle is said to be haunted.

8 Fortaleza de la Cabaña (1763–74)
MAP X1
When completed, this was the largest fortress in the Americas.

9 Fuerte Matachín (1802)
MAP R5
Protecting Baracoa from pirates, this castle still has cannons in situ.

10 Fuerte de la Loma (1869–75)
MAP N4
This fort guarded Puerto Padre during the Wars of Independence.

Santería

1 Orishas

The many deities of *Santería* (a Cuban religion with roots in west Africa) act as intermediaries between human beings and the supreme god, Olorún. Most *orishas* are avatars of Catholic saints, and each has his or her own costume, colors, symbols, and favorite foods, as well as specific abilities. Each believer has a personal *orisha*, who is considered to have the power over that person's destiny and is worshipped in daily life.

2 Santeros

Santeros are practitioners, initiated formally into *Santería,* and are believed to be possessed by their personal *orisha* who guides them to a better life. *Santeros* wear metal bracelets and colorful necklaces, which represent their particular *orisha*.

3 Altars

Altars are decorated with the attributes of the *orisha*, including their image in the form of a doll, devotional objects, and *ebó* (offerings). Tiny bells, maracas, and *agogó* (rattles) are played to awaken the *orisha*.

Ceramic and wood *Santería* symbols

Sacred *elekes* made of colored beads

4 Elekes

These necklaces of colored beads relate to specific *orishas*. While the uninitiated wear generic *elekes*, the bead patterns are determined by *santeros*, who prepare these necklaces using divination to find an order that reflects the *iyawó's* (initiate's) path.

5 Obi

Santería adherents believe that the wisdom of the *orishas* can be divined by dropping four pieces of coconut shell and studying the pattern they form. *Mojubas* (prayers) are said to invite the *orisha* to speak. These *obi* (oracles) are considered to help the believer reach wise decisions. At times, sacred palm seeds or cowrie shells are cast to invoke other oracles.

6 Initiation Ceremonies

Believers who seek a new path in life make a pact of veneration and obedience with their *orisha* through a week-long series of rituals. These require rigid adherence to meet the *orisha*'s approval. The final initiation usually involves animal sacrifice. For a year thereafter, the *iyawó* will adhere to strict prescriptions of behavior and dress solely in white.

7 Ebó

Santería rites, known as *ebó*, require offerings of food and drink to the *orishas*. An *ebó* often involves ritual cleansing, and may include sacrificing chickens, pigeons, or goats. *Ebó* is also used to woo an *orisha*'s favor, or protect practitioners against witchcraft.

⑧ Wemilere

These ritual ceremonies are held to honor *orishas*. They comprise prayers, songs, and *batá* drumming. A believer may sometimes go into a trance – he or she is then believed to be possessed by the *orisha*.

⑨ Babalawos

Babalawos are the powerful high priests of *Santería*, and act as intermediaries to interpret the commands of the *orishas*. They use seashells, coconut husks, and seeds to divine the future and interpret the oracles. A *santero* might be required to train for a decade to reach the status of *babalawo*.

***Babalawo* interpreting the oracles**

⑩ Batá

Of Yoruba origin, the sacred, hourglass-shaped *batá* drums – *itotele*, *iya*, and *okonkolo* – are carved of solid wood. Each has a different size and pitch. The drums are used during most important ceremonies and have their own rituals pertaining to their use and care.

Playing *batá* drums

TOP 10 ORISHAS

Yemayá, the Virgin of Regla

1 Yemayá
The mother goddess is the giver of life and the protector of children and pregnant women.

2 Olorún
The principal god, often considered the androgynous sum of all divinity. He is the source of all spiritual energy.

3 Obatalá
The father of humankind represents wisdom and purity. He is androgynous and celebrates Our Lady of Mercy.

4 Ochún
The youngest *orisha*, Ochún is the sensual deity of fresh water as well as the goddess of love.

5 Changó
The hot-tempered hero-god of thunder and lightning represents virility. His symbol is a double-bladed axe.

6 Babalu Aye
Associated with healing, Babalu Aye wears rags, walks with a crutch, and is accompanied by his dog.

7 Eleggua
God of the crossroads, Eleggua opens or closes the way of life. Cuban drivers often place Eleggua's *elekes* in their cars for protection.

8 Oggun
God of metal and war, he fights battles on behalf of petitioners and is often depicted with a machete.

9 Osain
This celibate deity represents the forces of nature. All initiations require his presence.

10 Oyá
She controls the fate of the injured and is aligned with St Barbara.

Nature Trails

1 Valle de Viñales
MAP B2

Surrounded by *mogotes*, Valle de Viñales has the most dramatic scenery in Cuba. Local tour agencies offer specialist hiking excursions along mountain trails, including climbs to the summit of *mogotes*; an official guide is obligatory.

Beautiful Valle de Viñales

2 El Yunque
The unique flat-topped El Yunque mountain *(see p33)* can be accessed by trail from Baracoa for a climb accompanied by a compulsory guide. The rewards are the staggering panoramic view and a chance to spot endemic birds.

3 Península de Guanahacabibes
MAP A3 ■ Centro de Visitantes: La Bajada, Sandino ■ 4875 0366 ■ Adm

At the far western tip of Cuba, this slender peninsula is covered with a rare expanse of tropical dry forest – a protected habitat for *jutías*, *jabalís*, and over 170 bird species. For birding and visits to caves, there are the Cueva de las Perlas and Sendero del Bosque al Mar trails.

4 Finca La Belén
MAP L4 ■ 27 miles (43 km) SE of Camagüey ■ 3286 4349 ■ Adm for horseback and guided bird tours

A walk or horseback ride from this working farm, home to zebra and various cattle, leads through semi-deciduous woodland and montane forests that help protect the different types of endemic plants including a rare cactus species. Bird-watchers will have a field day spotting parrots, hummingbirds, and other colorful birds.

5 Las Terrazas
This mountain resort *(see p16)* is Cuba's premier ecotourism destination, with trails, waterfalls, springs, and coffee plantations surrounded by forest. Hotel La Moka *(see p130)* provides decent lodgings.

Mineral springs at Las Terrazas

Rock formations at Gran Parque Natural Topes de Collantes

6 Topes de Collantes

This resort complex on the southeast flank of the Sierra del Escambray (see p95) makes a perfect base for exploring the steep trails through scented pine forests. The Parque Codina trail leads to an ancient coffee estate. Squawking parrots tear through the treetops, and the *tocororo* – Cuba's national bird (see p52) – can also often be spotted. Nearby, the El Nicho waterfall tumbles into crystal-clear pools.

7 Parque Nacional Desembarco del Granma

This dry, dusty park is the starting point for several recommended trails that take visitors through a cactus-studded tropical forest. Bird-watching is a big draw here, and manatees are sometimes seen in mangrove lagoons. The El Guafe trail leads to a large cave full of limestone formations (see p115).

8 Pinares de Mayarí

MAP P5 ■ 12 miles (19 km) S of Mayarí, Holguín province ■ 2445 5628

Take an excursion through a steep graded road to the wild pine-clad uplands of Pinares de Mayarí. This large area of montane wilderness is a popular base for guided hikes, such as the one to the Salto el Guayabo waterfall (see p116). A mountain resort that was created for the reigning Communist Party elite is now open to tourists.

9 Parque Nacional Alejandro Humboldt

Protecting the richest flora and fauna in Cuba, most of this wilderness is covered with dense rain-forest and mangroves along the shore. Trails range from easy walks to challenging climbs to the Balcón de Iberia waterfall (see p116).

Orchid at Parque Nacional Alejandro Humboldt

10 Pico Turquino

MAP N6 ■ Departure 8:15am ■ Adm permit including guides ■ Book visit at the Ecotur office, Hotel Sierra Maestra: Carretera Central, km 1.5, Bayamo; 2348 7006, comercial@grm.ecotur.tur.cu

Cuba's highest mountain can be ascended from either north or south sides, the most popular starting point being Santo Domingo. At least two days are required, and guides are compulsory for the climb. Prearrange a second set of guides if you plan to traverse the mountain.

Animals and Birds

Cuban amazon parrot

1 Cuban Amazon Parrot

The *cotorra*, or Cuban amazon parrot, an inhabitant of dry forests, was once found throughout Cuba. Now threatened, it is most easily seen in the Zapata swamps, on Isla de la Juventud, and in Parque Nacional Alejandro Humboldt. It performs noisy mating displays during the onset of the wet season.

2 Cuban Crocodile

Up to 16 ft (5 m) in length, the Cuban crocodile is endemic to the island and is far more aggressive than its cousin, the American crocodile, which is also found here. Despite being hunted to near extinction, the population has recovered thanks to a breeding program introduced by Fidel Castro.

3 Iguana

Resembling a small dragon, this leathery reptile inhabits offshore cays and feasts on leaves, fruit, and, occasionally, insects. It basks in the sun to become active, but seeks refuge from the mid-afternoon heat in cool burrows.

Rock Iguana

4 Solenodon

You are unlikely to see one of these long-nosed, ant-eating mammals in the wild, as they are shy and nocturnal. Resembling a giant shrew, the solenodon is an endangered species, as it is easy prey for dogs and mongooses.

5 Tocororo

This member of the trogon family is a pigeon-sized, forest-dwelling bird. The *tocororo* is Cuba's national bird because its blue, white, and red plumage corresponds to the colors of the nation's flag. It has a serrated bill, concave-tipped tail, and is common throughout the island.

6 Flamingo

With legs that resemble carnation stalks this pink bird is the most attractive of Cuba's many estuary birds. Large flocks of flamingos inhabit the saltwater lagoons of Zapata. They primarily eat insect larvae, which contain a substance that gives them their bright color.

7 Polymita

These snails are remarkable for their colorful shells, whorled in patterns unique to each individual. The shells of these multicolored

Extraordinary polymita

mollusks range from simple black-and-white spirals to blazing stripes of orange, yellow, and maroon. Unfortunately, these snails are now endangered due to the collection of their shells for tourist souvenirs.

8 Zunzuncito

The tiny Cuban hummingbird is so small, it is often mistaken for a bee, earning it the nickname "bee hummer." In fact, at only one inch (2.5 cm) long, it is the world's smallest bird. Nonetheless, this feisty bird defends its territory aggressively and has even been seen attacking vultures.

A *jutía* or tree rat

9 Jutía

A shy arboreal rat, the endemic *jutía* looks like an overgrown guinea pig. This rabbit-sized herbivore is endangered by deforestation, illegal hunting, and predators. It inhabits many of the wilderness regions of Cuba, but is most likely to be seen in captivity. Many Cubans breed *jutías* for food.

10 Jabalí

The Cuban wild boar is known for its highly aggressive nature when threatened. Covered in thick bristles, it is common to lowland wilderness areas. The *jabalí* is hunted for sport – its meat is a local delicacy.

TOP 10 CUBAN TREES AND FLOWERS

1 Royal Palm
Cuba's towering national tree is a beautiful palm with feather-like fronds.

2 Ceiba
This tree, with a huge limbless trunk topped by wide-spreading boughs, is attributed with magical-religious powers by believers of *Santería*.

3 Jagüey
Seeding atop host trees, this species drops roots to the ground and envelopes and chokes its host.

4 Sea Grape
This hardy shrub grows along shores and features broad, circular leaves and bunches of grape-like fruit.

5 Orchid
Hundreds of orchid species grow in Cuba from the plains to the mountains.

6 Creolean Pine
Native to the Caribbean, this species is found above about 5,000 ft (1,524 m).

7 Mariposa
The fragrant, white-petalled white ginger is Cuba's national flower and is known on the island as mariposa (butterfly) due to its shape.

8 Flamboyán
Flowering flame-red, this wide-spreading tree emblazons the country in spring and summer.

9 Cork Palm
The endangered cork palm grows only in remote areas of the Cordillera de Guaniguanico (see p87).

10 Mangrove
Five species of mangroves grow along Cuba's shores, rising from the waters on a tangle of interlocking stilts.

Mangroves

⏎🔟 Beaches

1 Playas del Este
MAP H4

Meandering for several miles east of Havana, this sweeping stretch of beaches is popular with the capital's citizens as a weekend hangout. Pounding surf and a powerful under-tow can be a deterrent to swimmers. The prettiest sections are Playa Santa María and Playa El Mégano, with gorgeous white sands and some beach facilities.

The pure white sands of Cayo Levisa

2 Cayo Levisa
MAP C2

This small island, ringed by white sands, an offshore coral reef, and mangroves, is renowned for its scuba diving. Coconut trees sway enticingly over a resort that has deluxe beachfront cabins along gorgeous white sands and turquoise waters.

3 Playa Sirena, Cayo Largo
MAP E4

Only a few miles from the all-inclusive hotels of Cayo Largo (see p86) this is a broad swathe of pure white sand with thatched restaurants. The waters are an alluring blue and perfect for watersports. Many tourists come to bask on the sands of this resort island. The water does get deep quickly, so children should be supervised at all times.

4 Playa Mayor, Varadero
MAP F1

Lined with hotels and beach-hut restaurants for almost its entire 7-mile (11.5-km) length, this long stretch of golden sand is the most well-developed beach in Cuba. Still, there is enough space for everyone, and the peacock-blue waters are shallow, safe for children, warm, and inviting.

5 Playa Esmeralda, Guardalavaca
MAP P4

Lying on the indented Atlantic coastline of Holguín province, Emerald Beach is truly a jewel. When you tire of the sands, wander along the ecological trails that lead through a mangrove and dry forest preserve, or take in the local sights.

6 Playa de los Flamencos, Cayo Coco

One of the most beautiful beaches in the country, Playa de los Flamencos

Playa de los Flamencos

sea lice that sometimes infest the waters and can result in the occurrence of flu-like infections.

8 Playa Pilar, Cayo Guillermo
MAP K1

Brushed by near-constant breezes, the white sands of this beach are swept into dunes overlooking pristine reef-protected waters, where you can wade knee-deep for 400 yards (366 m). Water birds can be found in the lagoons and mangroves, as well as hungry mosquitoes.

9 Playa Periquillo, Cayo Santa María
MAP J1

A long *pedraplén* (causeway) arcs across a shallow lagoon to reach the low-lying Playa Periquillo bay. The slender beach has pure white sands and warm waters. The shallows offer excellent bonefishing, while coral reefs and a wreckage are perfect for diving enthusiasts.

10 Playa Maguana
MAP P6

A gorgeous, custard-cream curve of sand about 12 miles (20 km) north of Baracoa. Come for the day and visit the cafés serving up fresh fish and cocktails by the beach. Locals also sell *cucuruchos*, a local delicacy. There's a small hotel at one end of the beach.

boasts white sand and turquoise waters protected by an offshore coral reef. With half a dozen large, beach-front hotels, the facilities here continue to expand as new hotels are added. However, there is plenty of wilderness as well. Wildlife, including the flamingos from whom the beach gets its name, parade around the inshore lagoons *(see p24)*.

7 Playa Ancón
MAP H4

Shaded by Australian pine, this white-sand beach lying along the Ancón Peninsula is within a 20-minute drive of Trinidad *(see p20)*. The Cuban government is in the process of gradually developing it as a tourist resort and several hotels and a diving school are found here. The Caribbean seas offer superb snorkeling and diving, but swimmers need to watch out for the microscopic

Playa Ancón's magnificent 2.5-mile (4-km) sweep of white sand

TOP 10 Children's Attractions

Steam train, unique to Cuba

1 Steam Train Rides

Once a vital resource for hauling sugarcane, many of Cuba's steam trains are now retired as museum pieces. Others are used for excursions at Central Australia (see p19) and at the Museo de Azúcar in Morón. Kids can also whistle down the tracks on a 1907 "choo-choo" that circles Havana's Parque Lenin in the summer months.

2 Cueva del Indio

MAP B2 ■ Carretera Puerto Esperanza, km 36 ■ 4879 6280 ■ Open 9am–4:45pm ■ Adm

This underground cavern in the Valle de San Vicente will delight children with its spooky, bat-ridden stalagmites and stalactites. The main thrill is a boat ride on an underground river that emerges into open air. Horseback rides are also offered (see p17).

3 Acuario Nacional

MAP F5 ■ Avenida 3ra & Calle 62, Miramar, Havana ■ 7202 5872 ■ Open 10am–4pm Tue–Sun ■ Adm

The outdoor National Aquarium in Havana features a large number of mammals, reptiles, birds, and fish.

4 Crocodile Farms

Kids can safely get close to crocodiles in breeding farms found on the island (see p88). Two farms breed the Cuban crocodile (which can grow to 16 ft/5 m long) while five breed the American species. Crocodiles are kept apart by age.

5 Music Matinees

Children of all ages will love the thrill of live music in Cuba. Look for matinee shows of salsa, rumba, and performances by singer-song-writers, especially in Havana, Santa Clara, and Santiago de Cuba.

6 Valle de la Prehistoria, Santiago de Cuba

Huge *Tyrannosaurus rex* occupy this prehistoric theme park, featuring life-size concrete reptiles. A natural history museum has informative displays on local wildlife (see p114).

Valle de la Prehistoria, Santiago de Cuba

(7) Horse-Drawn Carriages
MAP F2 ▪ Parque Josone, Avenida 1ra, Varadero

Enjoy the sights of La Habana Vieja or Varadero aboard an elegant horse-drawn carriage as it clip-clops through cobbled streets.

(8) El Morro, Santiago de Cuba

This ancient castle with impressive clifftop battlements comes alive at dusk, with a daily ceremony that sees real-life members of the Cuban military, dressed in the costumes of Independence soldiers, marching into the castle to fire a ceremonial cannon. The castle also displays a fine collection of muskets, swords, and other armaments from yesteryear (see p30).

El Morro, Santiago de Cuba

(9) Parque Recreativo Finca de Los Monos
MAP G5 ▪ Avenida de Santa Catalina corner of Calzada de Palatino, Cerro ▪ 7621 1961 ▪ Open 9am–6pm Thu–Sun

Once an estate with the world's largest private reserve of primates, today this tech park is home to electronic games, parkland, and an ice-cream parlor inside an aeroplane.

(10) Baseball
Estadio Latinoamericano: Calle Consejero Arango & Pedro Pérez, Cerro, Havana ▪ 7873 5479

Older children will enjoy the buzz of an evening baseball game. It is a spectacle accompanied by lots of music and cheering, and the games often end late at night.

TOP 10 ATTRACTIONS FOR CHILDREN IN HAVANA

Children in-line skating in Prado

1 Prado
A great place to interact with Cuban children who enjoy in-line skating.

2 Acuario Nacional
Children are enthralled by the tropical species on display at the National Aquarium.

3 Cañonazo
MAP X1
Soldiers fire a cannon at 9pm every evening from El Morro fortress.

4 Shadow Puppetry
MAP X5 ▪ Av. del Puerto & Obrapía ▪ 7801 1568
El Arca (The Ark) puppet museum and theater puts on delightful shows.

5 Horseback Rides
Kids can mount horses in Parque Lenin or Parque Luz y Caballero, one block north of Plaza de la Catedral.

6 Planetario
MAP X5 ▪ Plaza Vieja ▪ 7801 8544
A smart tour around the solar system with high tech gadgetry.

7 Playas del Este
These family-friendly beaches outside Havana have warm waters (see p54).

8 Teatro Guiñol
MAP U1 ▪ Calle M & 17 ▪ 7832 6262
This theater in Vedado has comedy and marioneta (puppet) shows.

9 Museo del Chocolate
MAP X5 ▪ Calle Mercaderes y Amargura ▪ 7866 4431
More café than museum, this is where visitors can watch chocolate being made and taste what's on offer.

10 Trompoloco Circus
Calle 112, Playa ▪ 7206 5609
Clowns and acrobats perform beneath a huge circus tent.

TOP 10 Musical Styles

A group of Cuban musicians play *son* in a shaded plaza, Trinidad

1 Son

Initially becoming popular in the second half of the 19th century in the eastern province of Oriente, *son* peaked in the 1950s. It was revived decades later by the *Buena Vista Social Club* movie and album.

2 Classical

Cuba has a National Symphony Orchestra and many smaller accomplished ensembles sponsored by the government. A unique style has evolved, known as *Afrocubanismo*, which incorporates African-derived instruments and rhythms into classical themes.

Cuban jazz performer

3 Jazz

A musical form that has made a resounding comeback in Cuba in recent years, jazz was suppressed following the Revolution *(see p37)*. A fast-paced Afro-Cuban style has emerged, propelling Cuban musicians to the fore of the world jazz scene, and the Havana Festival de Jazz Plaza is a major event in the musical calendar.

4 Danzón

Originating in France via Haiti in the 18th century, *danzón* is the root source of most Cuban music, and gained popularity within enslaved communities and with agricultural workers. Played by *orquestras típicas*, *danzón* has a repetitive jaunty tempo, and is the Cuban national dance.

5 Changüí

A rougher variant of *son*, *changüí* has minimal instrumentation with the *tres* (similar to a guitar) and *bongos* dominating. It is played mainly in the eastern provinces, notably by groups such as the Estrellas Campesinas and Grupo Changüí.

Brass section of a classical orchestra

6 Guaguancó

Born in the slave *barracoons* of 18th-century sugar estates, this folkloric Afro-Cuban dance is highly flirtatious. Accompanied by complex bongo rhythms, the male dancer circles his female partner, who dances in a provocative yet defensive manner in front of him.

7 Timba

A derivative of salsa, the highly aggressive and innovative *timba* is an eclectic and evolving musical form that incorporates various genres, including classical, disco, and even hip hop. Improvisation is key to this flexible form.

8 Rumba

Social gatherings in Cuba often evolve into informal *rumbas*, a generic term which covers a variety of African-derived rhythms and dances involving sensuous flicks of the hips. Many rumbas involve a call-and-answer pattern between singers and drummers.

Rumba dancers

9 Salsa

A popular form that evolved in the 1960s, when Cuban musicians began experimenting with new sounds and styles from the US. Fusing jazz and rock with traditional *son*, it is normally fast and intense, but can also be slow and romantic.

10 Rap

Cuba's contemporary rap scene differs markedly from its aggressive US counterpart. *Raperos* use rap to express their frustrations and focus on socio-political commentary with the intention of bettering society.

TOP 10 MUSICIANS

Remarkable Chucho Valdés

1 Chucho Valdés (b.1941)
This Grammy award-winning jazz pianist is considered to be one of the world's greats.

2 Compay Segundo (1907–2003)
Sentimental guitarist of the 1940s, Segundo's career was resurrected with the *Buena Vista Social Club* movie.

3 Frank Fernández (b.1944)
Cuba's foremost classical pianist and composer studied at Moscow's Tchaikovsky Conservatory.

4 Celia Cruz (1925–2003)
Legendary salsa singer who left Cuba in 1960 and found fame in the US.

5 Benny Moré (1919–63)
This tenor sang everything from *son* to *mambo* and is considered perhaps the greatest Cuban singer of all.

6 Juan Formell (1942–2014)
Founder of Orquesta Revé and Los Van Van – Cuba's most popular salsa band.

7 Silvio Rodríguez (b.1946)
The foremost exponent of politicized *nueva trova* ballads, also a former member of parliament.

8 Gonzalo Rubalcaba (b.1963)
This contemporary jazz pianist performs in concerts all over the world and is a Grammy award winner.

9 Pablo Milanés (b.1943)
A singer-songwriter of *nueva trova*, this guitarist hails from the city of Bayamo.

10 Omara Portuondo (b.1930)
A renowned singer since the 1950s, she starred in the Buena Vista Social Club and still performs worldwide.

TOP 10 Places to Meet the Locals

Locals and tourists alike gathering on the white sands of Playas del Este

1 Playas del Este
On weekends, families flee sticky Havana for a day at the beach. Tourists usually gather toward the west end, though many Cuban families prefer the beach around Guanabo *(see p54)*.

2 Parque Central, Havana
Havana has many plazas, but this tree-shaded park on the edge of Old Havana is the liveliest. Baseball fans gather here to argue the finer points of the game. With plenty of benches, it is a great place to watch the flurry of activity. Expect *jineteros* (hustlers) to approach you to tout their wares or services *(see p125)*.

3 The Malecón, Havana
The cooling breezes of the capital's seafront esplanade attracts *habaneros* (Havana locals) of all ages, who socialize with guitars and bottles of rum. On hot days families bathe in the *balnearios* cut into the limestone rock. It's the perfect place for a sunset stroll but take care and be sure to watch your step – the sidewalk is crumbling and waves often crash right over the seawall *(see p14)*.

4 Casas de la Trova
When bitten by the dancing bug, head to a Casa de la Trova. Every town has one of these traditional live music houses, where Cuban singles as well as couples have a great time dancing to salsa and timeless *sons* and *boleros*.

5 Calle Obispo, Havana
This pedestrian-only shopping street has plenty of intriguing shops, bars, cafés, and ice-cream stores. It is also packed with many private art galleries *(see p80)*. Pickpockets are on the prowl, so make sure you guard your belongings.

Calle Obispo, Havana

6 Baseball Games
Watching a Cuban baseball game is as much a social experience as a sporting one. The crowds are passionate but friendly, and the game is interspersed with chatting and drinking. You will make new friends here, even if you support the "other" team.

7 Cumbanchas
Cubans are passionate about music and dance and many spark up their own song and dance at street parties where anyone can join in. Contribute a bottle of rum, the drink of choice, as courtesy. Even if you arrive with a partner, expect to be asked to dance.

8 Coppelia
Cubans adore ice cream, and every major town has an outlet selling the Coppelia brand. Seating is communal and ice cream is sold at incredibly low prices. Standing in line with Cubans is part of the experience. The branch in Havana is spread over an entire block (see p79).

Mercados Agropecuarios, Havana

9 Mercados Agropecuarios
The farmers' markets are packed with Cubans shopping for fresh produce, while others enjoy the local gossip. Every town has at least one "agro." Even if you are not planning to buy, the atmosphere makes a visit worthwhile.

10 Casas de la Cultura
These cultural centers can be found in every town. The atmosphere is informal and they are great places to make new friends and perhaps learn a few dance moves.

TOP 10 CUSTOMS AND BELIEFS

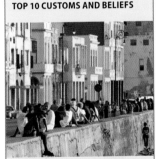

Taking it easy on the Malecón

1 Take it Easy
Hurrying is uncommon in Cuba, and foreigners who expect things to happen quickly can be disappointed.

2 Politeness
Common courtesies, such as saying "thank you" and "please," are very important to Cuban people.

3 Dress
Cubans dress fairly conventionally. Anyone wearing alternative clothing may be viewed as anti-establishment.

4 Santería
More than half the Cuban population are followers of this Afro-Cuban religion (see pp48–9).

5 Superstitions
Superstitious beliefs relating to dreams, money, luck or warding off evil spirits permeate the lives of many Cubans.

6 Equality
The concept of equality for all on every level is a concept Cubans hold very close to their hearts.

7 Greetings
Cubans greet everyone upon entering a room. Revolutionaries refer to each other as *compañero* (companion).

8 Machismo
Some Cuban men are known to flirt openly.

9 "The New Man"
Che Guevara dreamed of creating a society where people were motivated by altruism.

10 Chistes (Jokes)
A great sense of humor helps many Cubans deal with the hardships of daily life – the subject of most *chistes*.

🔟 Cuban Dishes

4 Corvina al Ajillo

This simple and delicious dish of seabass with a garlic sauce is typically combined with slices of lime and regular vegetables such as carrots. Usually either mashed potatoes or *moros y cristianos* are served on the side.

5 Pollo con Quimbombó

A traditional country recipe, this dish is a chicken casserole simmered with chopped okra, onions, garlic, green pepper, and tomato, plus plantain and seasoned with black pepper, coriander, and lime juice. It is served with a bowl of steamed or boiled *malanga* (a starchy root vegetable), yams, and potatoes, along with white rice.

Cerdo Asado (succulent roast pork)

1 Cerdo Asado

Pork is roasted in an open oven or on a spit, and is served whole or sliced. *Cerdo Asado* is usually served with rice and black beans accompanied by fried plantain.

2 Moros y Cristianos

The base of *comida criolla* (traditional Cuban fare), this dish comprises white rice cooked with black beans and is served as an accompaniment to meat and seafood meals. It is known as *congrí* when cooked with red beans and *congrí oriental* when the red and black beans are mixed.

Moros y Cristianos

3 Bistec Uruguayo

"Uruguayan beef," a staple found on many restaurant menus, is a steak stuffed with ham and cheese. It is usually accompanied by a side salad of boiled vegetables, mashed potatoes or rice, and beans. Fish and chicken are often used instead of beef.

6 Potaje

Black beans are slow-cooked with garlic, onions, pepper, oregano, and other herbs to produce this delicious, thick soup. Sometimes pieces of pork or chicken are added. A bowl of plain white rice is usually the sole accompaniment.

7 Ajiaco

This minestrone-style vegetable stew is made with *malanga*, turnips, corn, and yucca, plus a variety of meats, including pork and chicken. It is seasoned with herbs.

Ajiaco, a popular Cuban stew

Classic Cuban flan

⑧ Flan
Cuba's most popular dessert, apart from ice cream, this is found on most menus. It closely resembles *crème caramel.* A sweet custard made from eggs and milk is baked over a caramelized sugar base, which, when the dish is turned out, provides a delicious sauce.

⑨ Ropa Vieja
"Old clothes" is a delicious combination of boiled rice, black beans, fried plantain, and shredded beef marinated in red wine or rum, seasoned with onions, peppers, oregano, and cumin.

Ropa Vieja

⑩ Enchilada de Langosta
Lobster is typically boiled, then cooked in a sauce of tomatoes and spiced with peppers and other seasonings. Shrimp is often used as a substitute for lobster. It is usually served with rice and a salad of lettuce and boiled vegetables.

TOP 10 DRINKS

Ice-cold mojitos

1 Mojito
This world-famous Cuban drink is made of white rum with mint leaves, sugar, and a dash of soda water.

2 Cuba Libre
Dark rum with cola and natural lime juice served with plenty of ice in a tall glass, garnished with a lime.

3 Cristal
A light, lager-style beer, usually served chilled. It has a milder taste than the more full-bodied Bucanero beer.

4 Rum
Younger "white" rums are used for most cocktails, while aged rums – *añejos* – are typically drunk straight.

5 Daiquirí
White rum blended with sugar, lime juice, and crushed ice, and served in a broad glass decorated with a maraschino cherry.

6 Fruit Juices
Many tropical fruits are packaged as fresh juices, including *guayaba* (guava), grapefruit, and orange.

7 Batidos
Water or milk is blended with ice and fresh fruit, such as mango and papaya, to make a refreshing shake.

8 Refrescos
An infinite variety of tropical fruit-flavored, water-based, sweetened drinks, often carbonated.

9 Pru
Made from various herbs and roots, this medicinal drink is served in the eastern provinces of Cuba.

10 Chorote
Strongly flavored chocolate drink of Baracoa, thickened with cornstarch and sweetened with sugar.

🔟 Things to Buy

Painted fan souvenirs, Havana

1 Fans

Traditional, handmade, and prettily painted Spanish fans or *abanicos* make a great gift. The fans are hand-painted in an age-old tradition. Gift shops throughout Cuba also sell them.

2 Guayaberas

This iconic Cuban cotton shirt was first created in Sancti Spíritus. Worn by men, Guayabera is ideal for beating the heat. It features a straight hem and is worn draped outside the trousers. Either long- or short-sleeved, the shirts usually have four buttoned pockets and are embroidered with twin vertical stripes down the front. The Casa de la Guayabera *(Calle El Llano y Padre Quintero)* displays more than 200 of these shirts, some of which have been worn by people like Fidel Castro and Colombian novelist Gabriel García Márquez.

3 Papier-Mâché Models

Cuban artisans are skilled at making papier-mâché items, and pre-revolutionary American automobiles are a very popular theme. These cars can be incredibly lifelike or have comical distortions. Look out as well for papier-mâché *muñequitas* (dolls) of the *orishas*, or figures of baseball players, and women.

4 Accessories

Havana's new wave of designers sell a host of gifts in indie shops, including stylish clothes, bags, footwear and unique jewelry.

5 Music CDs

CDs of everything from *son* and jazz to *timba* and salsa are widely available in *casas de la trova (see p60)*, souvenir stores, and shops run by the state-owned recording entity EGREM. Musicians who perform at restaurants and other venues often offer recordings of their music for sale.

6 Wood Carvings

Carved wooden statues are a staple of craft markets found all over Cuba. The most common items, which make good souvenirs or gifts, are exaggeratedly slender nude female figures made of mahogany, ebony, and *lignum vitae*. Bowls and plates are also available, as are chess sets and humidors, often made in colorful combinations of different types of hardwoods.

Wooden carvings at a street market

7 Coffee

Some of the best mountain-grown beans in the Caribbean are sold in vacuum-sealed packages at reasonable prices. Many shops sell a rich, smooth export-quality brand called Cubanita.

8 Cuban Art

Although much Cuban art is kitsch and mass-produced for tourists, the nation's many artists also produce some of the most visually exciting works in the Caribbean. Colorful recreations of typical street scenes featuring old American automobiles or ox-drawn carts are irresistible, but also look for more profound works by contemporary masters. The former are sold at street markets nationwide; the latter are represented at quality state-run galleries, and in art spaces.

Cuban art on display

9 Jewelry

Scour the street markets for creative avant-garde pieces. Some makers use recycled cutlery, plastics, and other reused materials. To really dive into the jewelry scene, visit the indie boutiques Jorge Gil and La Libertija in Old Havana, and Alma in Miramar.

10 Lace

Much of Cuba's beautiful, traditional lace embroidery is from Trinidad, the center of homespun production. Look for exquisite table-cloths, antimacassars, and blouses, as well as pretty, crocheted bikinis.

TOP 10 RUMS AND CIGARS

1 Ron Matusalem Añejo
Elegant rum aged in barrels for 10 years, three years longer than most *añejos*.

2 Montecristo No. 4
The world's top-selling cigar; the preferred smoke of Che Guevara.

3 Cohiba Siglo
Large, flawless cigar loaded with flavor.

4 Varadero Oro
Aged for five years, this dark golden rum is smooth, sweet, and has distinctive caramel flavors.

5 Partagás Series D
A full-bodied cigar with an intense, earthy flavor, this Robusto is the standard-bearer of the Partagás brand.

Cohiba Siglo

6 Montecristo Figurados No. 2
This extremely rare, perfectly balanced, distinctly flavored, torpedo-shaped cigar is sought after by connoisseurs.

7 Ron Santiago 45 Aniversario
A limited-edition, well-aged rum with hints of honey and walnuts – one of Cuba's finest.

8 Romeo y Julieta Churchill
This long, large, full-bodied smoke is named after Shakespeare's tragic play and British premier Winston Churchill.

9 Trinidad Fundadores
A classic, considered perhaps the finest of Cuban cigars. Fidel Castro presented these to visiting dignitaries.

10 Havana Club Gran Reserva
Aged for 15 years, this is one of the finest Cuban rums, with a texture and flavor like a superb cognac.

Havana Club rum

🔟 Cuba for Free

Catedral de La Habana

1 Churches
Although most museums have an admission charge, Cuba is replete with ancient churches that are free to enter such as the exquisite Baroque Catedral de La Habana (see p73), and the Basílica de Nuestra de Señora de la Caridad del Cobre (see p113), just outside Santiago de Cuba.

2 La Habana Vieja
Havana's greatest freebie happens to be a must-see attraction with a handful of colonial plazas and dozens of bustling streets to explore. Don't miss Catedral de La Habana, the Plaza de Armas (see p72), Plaza Vieja (see p73), and Parque Central (see p75) – the epicenter of social life – surrounded by astonishing buildings.

3 The Malecón
On any evening, and especially on weekends, Havana's seafront boulevard becomes an impromptu party scene. Thousands of young Cubans sit on the sea wall to watch the sunset, flirt, listen to music, and share bottles of rum. By day you'll find skateboarders, in-line skaters, fishermen, musicians, and always romantic couples (see p76).

4 Beach Resorts
Not all Cuba's beaches are free. Those accessed by *pedraplén* (see p25) charge a fee for use of the causeway. But other scintillating white sands, such as those of Playas del Este (see p54) and Varadero, are free, and there's never a charge for enjoying the warm turquoise seas.

5 Casa de la Trovas
Every town has a traditional music house where you can enjoy live music and dance to your heart's content. Many offer afternoon as well as evening activities, usually free of charge. It's a great way to strike up friendships with Cubans (see p60). The best and most interesting casas are those in Trinidad and Santiago de Cuba (see p115).

6 Colonial Trinidad
Simply strolling the cobbled streets of this colonial gem will immerse you in a quintessential Cuban experience (see pp20–21). Many private art spaces line the plazas, and the Iglesia Parroquial de la Santísima Trinidad (see p106) can be enjoyed for free, as can such nearby attractions as the Valle de los Ingenios (see p103), with its fascinating ruined sugar mills.

Visitors relaxing along The Malecón

7 Plaza de la Revolución

Although there's a fee for the museum beneath the giant monument to the much-loved José Martí, this massive plaza *(see p74)* in the heart of Havana is surrounded by impressive sights, including the giant steel Che Guevara mural dominating the Ministerio del Interior. A convertible classic car taxi is the most stylish atmospheric way to arrive in the plaza, but the Havana BusTour also stops here *(see pp120–21)*.

Steel mural in Plaza de la Revolución

8 Free Festivals

Fancy mingling with locals at one of the many annual festivals *(see pp68–9)* in Cuba? You can let your hair down in the revelry of Carnaval in Santiago de Cuba; enjoy the thrilling firework spectacle of Remedios' year-end *parranda*; or even show solidarity during the Día de los Trabajadores (Day of the Workers).

9 Casas de la Cultura

Meet local artists, musicians, poets, and writers in community centers known as Casas de la Cultura, found all over the country *(see p61)*. Enjoy cultural activities such as live performances, music shows, art exhibitions, and dance classes – almost everything they put on is free.

10 Bandstands

Most big towns in Cuba have a central square with bandstands, where local bands perform for free, usually on weekend nights. Sit on a bench or grab someone's hand and join the locals in these wonderful expressions of community spirit.

TOP 10 BUDGET TIPS

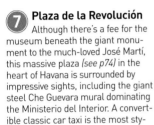

Casa particular **interior**

1 Havana BusTour takes in most of Havana's top sights for the price of a single all-day fare. With dozens of stops along the route, it is a complete sightseeing experience of the city.

2 Take advantage of the good-value set cajita lunches that are sold at roadside stalls.

3 Stay at casas *particulares*, which offer great value and give you insight into how Cuban families live.

4 Join the Cubans in line at Coppelia and pay for your ice cream in pesos, rather than buying ice cream in hard currency elsewhere. Most large cities have a Coppelia outlet.

5 Buy a ticket for both sections of the Museo de Bellas Artes, as the Cuban and International sections charge more if you pay separately.

6 Rather than taking relatively expensive taxis, travel by public bus or hop into a *colectivo* taxi for longer journeys within cities.

7 Comb through the book fair off the southeast corner of Plaza de Armas for rare posters and other unique retro finds *(see p72)*.

8 Bring Euro notes as it is considered one of the strongest foreign currencies in Cuba.

9 Go gallery-hopping in Trinidad, where dozens of roadside stores sell artwork of surprisingly good quality.

10 Outside of Havana, you can catch theatre, music, and dance performances for free or at very low cost.

Festivals and Holidays

1 Jan 1, Liberation Day
New Year's Day in Cuba is celebrated as the day that dictator Fulgencio Batista (see p43) was toppled. Officially known as the "Anniversary of the Triumph of the Revolution," the event is marked by nationwide musical concerts.

2 Jan 28, José Martí's Birthday
Cubans celebrate the birth of Martí (see p37) with events including readings of his much admired poetry and concerts and a candle-lit procession.

Children on José Martí's birthday

held throughout the island, as Cubans proclaim their dedication to socialism and the Revolution.

3 Apr 19, Victoria de Playa Girón
The plaza and museum behind the beach at Playa Girón is the setting for speeches, a wreath-laying ceremony, and festivities to celebrate the "first defeat of imperialism in the Americas." The holiday honors the Cuban victory in the Bay of Pigs invasion (see p37).

5 Jul 26, National Revolution Day
A celebration of the launch of the Revolution of 1953 (see p37) is held in a different city each year. Attendees dress in black and red T-shirts – the colors of Castro's revolutionary movement – and listen to speeches by Communist leaders.

4 May 1, Día de los Trabajadores
As many as half a million citizens march through Plaza de la Revolución (see p15), while Cuba's leaders look on. Rallies that include the singing of patriotic songs are

6 Jul, Carnaval
Many major cities organize a street carnival in July featuring live music and dancing. The biggest event is in Santiago de Cuba (see pp30–31), where carnival season climaxes with a parade of bands along Avenida Jesús Menéndez.

Revellers celebrating the Día de los Trabajadores

7 Oct 8, Anniversary of Che Guevara's death

Santa Clara's Plaza de la Revolución and the Monumento del Che (see p39) are the setting for a wreath-laying ceremony in the presence of key political leaders.

8 Oct 28, Memorial to Camilo Cienfuegos

Schoolchildren in Havana march to the Malecón (see p14) to throw "a flower for Camilo" into the sea on the anniversary of the death of Cienfuegos (see p41). This revolutionary commander went missing in 1959, when his plane disappeared during a night flight. There is also a parade to the sea at the Museo de Camilo Cienfuegos in Jaguajay, Sancti Spíritus province.

Ballet Nacional de Cuba

9 Nov, Festival de Ballet

For 10 days biennially at the end of October, Havana's Gran Teatro (see p77) plays host to brilliant ballet performances featuring leading international dancers and ballet corps. Hosted by the Ballet Nacional de Cuba, the festival is one of the major events in the cultural calendar.

10 Dec, Festival de Nuevo Cine Latinoamericano

Cubans are avid moviegoers, and the highlight of their year is the Latin American Film Festival, which screens a variety of art-house films and documentaries from around the world, as well as works from some of Cuba's own top directors.

TOP 10 LOCAL FESTIVALS

Parrandas in Remedios

1 Holguín (Jan), Semana de Cultura Holguinera
The town comes alive with a medley of cultural activities.

2 Camagüey (Feb), Jornadas de la Cultura Camagüeyana
This city celebrates its founding with much fanfare.

3 Trinidad (Easter), El Recorrido del Vía Cruce
Catholic devotees follow the ancient "way of the cross."

4 Las Tunas (Jun), Jornada Cucalambeana
Singers compete in *décimas* – ten-syllable rhyming verses – to honor this composer.

5 Cienfuegos (Aug), Festival de la Música Alternativa Cubana "Ciudad del Mar"
A celebration of alternative music that also pays homage to Benny Moré (see p59).

6 Santiago de Cuba (Aug), Festival de Pregón
Citizens converge on Parque Céspedes to recite traditional songs and verses.

7 Guantánamo (Dec), Festival del Changüí
Party as *son* groups perform (see p58).

8 Trinidad (Dec), Fiestas Navideñas
The journey of Mary and Joseph is re-created.

9 Rincón (Dec 17), Procesión de los Milagros
The *orisha* St Lazarus is honored in this pilgrimage.

10 Remedios (24–29 Dec), Parrandas
Two sides of town duel in a firework contest (see p95).

Cuba
Area by Area

Musicians in Trinidad

🔟 Havana

From the picturesque colonial district of La Habana Vieja (Old Havana) to the early 20th-century grandeur of Vedado, central Havana is full of appeal. Centered on four plazas, much of La Habana Vieja has

been restored and teems with atmospheric hotels, top restaurants, trendy boutiques, and hip bars. Vedado's grid of tree-shaded streets is lined with once-resplendent mansions. Attractions here include the Plaza de la Revolución, the setting for political marches past and present. Nightclubs from the area's 1950s heyday still sizzle, and high-rise hotels of the same era remain a popular draw.

Street sign

1 Plaza de Armas

This cobbled plaza (see p13), laid out in 1582 as the administrative center of Cuba, is named for the military exercises that took place here. It is surrounded by notable historic buildings, such as the Castillo de la Real Fuerza (see p47), the temple-like Neo-Classical El Templete, and the Cuban Baroque Palacio de los Capitanes Generales – a former governor's palace housing the insightful Museo de la Ciudad (see p46).

HAVANA

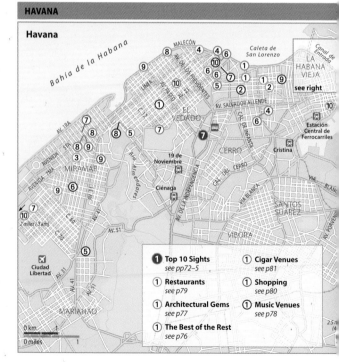

Havana

Bahía de la Habana

MALECÓN

Caleta de San Lorenzo

LA HABANA VIEJA

see right

EL VEDADO

AV. SALVADOR ALLENDE

Estación Central de Ferrocarriles

CERRO

Cristina

MIRAMAR

19 de Noviembre

Ciénaga

VÍA BLANCA

SANTOS SUÁREZ

VÍBORA

Ciudad Libertad

MARIANAO

2 miles (3 km)

0 km   1
0 miles   1

2.5 miles (4

❶ **Top 10 Sights** see pp72–5	❶ **Cigar Venues** see p81
❶ **Restaurants** see p79	❶ **Shopping** see p80
❶ **Architectural Gems** see p77	❶ **Music Venues** see p78
❶ **The Best of the Rest** see p76	

Colonial mansions surround the Catedral de La Habana

2 Catedral de La Habana

Havana's charming cathedral (1777), officially known as Catedral de la Virgen María de la Concepción Inmaculada and sometimes referred to as Catedral San Cristóbal, has an exquisite Baroque facade supported by pilasters and two asymmetrical bell towers. Restored frescoes by Giuseppe Perovani adorn the relatively austere altar. The cathedral stands on a plaza that is surrounded by colonial mansions (see p12).

3 Plaza Vieja

MAP X5 ■ Fototeca de Cuba: Calle Mercaderes 307; 7801 8141; open 10am–4pm Tue–Sat ■ Museo de Naipes: 7801 8132; open 9:30am–5pm Tue–Sat

Magnificent buildings spanning four centuries rise on each side of the square (see p12). The 18th-century building housing the Fototeca de Cuba has photography exhibitions; the Museo de Naipes displays a collection of playing cards.

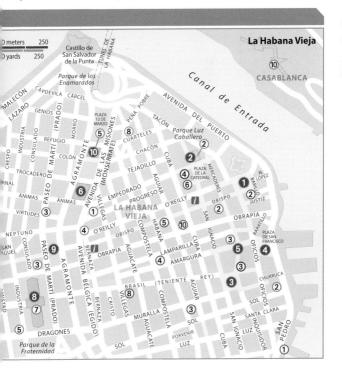

4 Plaza de San Francisco

This cobbled plaza formerly opened onto the harborfront. It is dominated by the Basílica Menor de San Francisco de Asís – a former cathedral that ceased to be used for worship following British occupation in 1762. Today it is a concert hall as well as a religious art museum. The plaza also features restored buildings spanning three centuries (see p12).

5 Calle Mercaderes

MAP X5 ■ Casa de Asia: Calle Mercaderes 111, La Habana Vieja; 7801 1740; open 9:30am–5pm Tue–Sat, 9:30am–12:30pm Sun ■ Museo del Tabaco: Calle Mercaderes 120, La Habana Vieja; 7861 5795; open 9:30am–5pm Tue–Sat, 9:30am–1pm Sun; adm ■ Maqueta del Centro Histórico: Calle Mercaderes 114, La Habana Vieja; 7866 4425; open 8:30am–6pm daily; adm

This cobbled street (see p12) is lined with colonial mansions housing tiny museums, boutiques, and other fascinating places. The three blocks might take a full morning to explore, with requisite stops at the Museo de Asia, Museo del Tabaco, and Maqueta del Centro Histórico – a fabulous scale-model of La Habana Vieja. Break your stroll at Mesón de la Flota, a *bodega* hosting live flamenco.

6 Museo Nacional de Bellas Artes

This world-class museum is in two parts. An international section occupies the Renaissance-style Centro Asturiano, built in 1927, and boasts treasures from Ancient Egypt, Greece, and Rome. There are also

RESTORING OLD HAVANA

In 1982, UNESCO recognized La Habana Vieja (below) as a World Heritage Site, and Cuba initiated a plan to save the crumbling colonial city. Eusebio Leal, the late Havana City Historian, oversaw the remarkable effort. Priority has been given to the most important buildings, many of which have been transformed into museums, hotels, and bars.

works by North American and European masters, including Gainsborough, Goya, and Rubens. The Modernist Palace of Fine Arts, a separate building two blocks away, displays works by Cuban artists from different periods (see p12).

7 Plaza de la Revolución

The administrative and political center of Cuba since the early 1950s, the plaza is surrounded with Modernist and monumentalist government buildings. Huge political rallies are held here. The Memorial José Martí on the south side features a large granite monument to the celebrated figure, plus an excellent museum topped by a Surrealist tower. A striking visage of Che Guevara adorns the facade of the Ministerio del Interior (see p15).

Museum within the Memorial José Martí in Plaza de la Revolución

8 Capitolio

The nation's grandiose former congressional building was inaugurated in 1929 and incorporates Art Deco elements into a Neo-Classical design that closely resembles Washington D. C.'s Capitol. Tastefully restored, and open to public visits, it is now home to the National Assembly. Visitors approach via a steep flight of stairs flanked by Neo-Classical bronze figures. Behind the central portico with its 12 granite columns are three bronze doors with bas-reliefs of major events of Cuban history. A huge Statue of the Republic stands at the entrance hall, which features a fake 25-carat diamond embedded in the floor *(see p14)*.

The grand Capitolio building

9 Parque Central

An epicenter of social life in Havana, this palm-shaded square has a statue of José Martí *(see p42)* and is surrounded by monumental 19th- and 20th-century buildings. These include the Neo-Classical Kempinski hotel and the spectacular Gran Teatro *(see p77)*.

10 Museo de la Revolución

Housed in the former presidential palace once occupied by General Batista, this museum *(see p13)* is a tribute to the Revolution, from the guerrilla war to the current day. The ornate, domed building, built in 1920, is as fascinating as the collection, and includes the Salón de los Espejos, a hall lined with mirrors. At the rear is the Granma Memorial *(see p38)*, featuring the yacht *Granma* as well as aircrafts and vehicles used in the Bay of Pigs invasion *(see p37)*.

LA HABANA VIEJA WALK

▶ MORNING

After breakfast, head to Plaza de la Catedral, the most intimate of the city's colonial plazas. Peek inside the **Catedral de La Habana** *(see p12)* and then stop for a drink at Ernest Hemingway's favorite haunt, **La Bodeguita del Medio** *(see p78)*. Stroll along Calle San Ignacio, passing its art galleries. Then turn left on Calle O'Reilly and walk two blocks south to **Plaza de Armas** *(see p13)*. Move around the square in a clockwise direction, stopping to admire the **Castillo de la Real Fuerza** *(see p47)*. On the park's eastern side, explore the **Palacio de los Capitanes Generales** *(see p12)*, before exiting the square along Calle Oficios. Take your time to admire the 18th-century buildings here.

AFTERNOON

Stop for refreshments at **La Imprenta**, a stylish restaurant on cobbled Calle Mercaderes *(No. 208)*. Revived, continue southeast to visit the **Basílica Menor de San Francisco de Asís** *(see p12)*, where you can scale the bell tower for great views over the harbor and La Habana Vieja. Then walk toward **Plaza Vieja** *(see p73)*, where highlights include the Museo de Naipes and the Cámara Oscura, a rooftop optical reflection camera that offers a magnified view of life from the top of Havana. End your day with a meal and chilled beer at **Factoría Plaza Vieja**, a brewpub on the plaza.

See map on pp72–3

The Best of the Rest

1 Malecón
MAP S2–W1

Connecting La Habana Vieja to Vedado, this seafront boulevard offers grand vistas and is a gathering spot for locals. Beware of dangerous potholes.

2 Fundación Havana Club
MAP T3 ■ Calle San Pedro 262, La Habana Vieja ■ 7861 8051 ■ Open 9am–4pm Mon–Fri ■ Adm (includes guided tour and drinks)

The Havana Club Foundation's lively museum educates visitors on rum production. A range of rums can be sampled at the bar.

3 Paseo de Martí
Known locally as "Prado," this is a tree-shaded promenade guarded by bronze lions. Here, children play and enjoy lessons as locals sit and chat *(see p14)*.

4 Fábrica de Tabacos H. Upmann
MAP V2 ■ Calle Belascoaín 852, Centro Habana ■ 7878 5966 ■ Open 9am–1pm Mon–Fri ■ Adm for guided tours (book in advance through a state tour agent)

This cigar factory dates back to 1875 and provides a fascinating glimpse into the art of cigar-making.

5 Universidad de La Habana
The city's university is home to Neo-Classical buildings, two museums, and a staircase that was the setting for several violent demonstrations in pre-revolutionary days *(see p14)*.

6 Hotel Nacional
MAP U1 ■ Calle O & 21 ■ 7836 3564

This imposing Neo-Classical 1930s hotel draws visitors with its lavish decor, various bars, and gardens.

7 Cementerio Colón
MAP S3–T3 ■ Av. Zapata & Calle 12, Vedado ■ 7830 4517 ■ Open 8am–5pm daily ■ Adm

One of the world's most astounding cemeteries, this massive necropolis features tombs representing a pantheon of important figures.

8 San Isidro Art District
MAP W6–X6 ■ Southern streets of Old Havana

Street artists have spray-painted art and murals across squares. Look out for art galleries, bars, and art festivals.

9 Museo Ernest Hemingway
MAP V3 ■ Calle Vigía, San Francisco de Paula ■ 7693 3419 ■ Open 10am–5pm Mon–Sat (closed when raining) ■ Adm

Hemingway's former home remains just as he left it *(see p47)*.

10 Parque Histórico-Militar Morro-Cabaña
MAP X1 ■ Carretera de la Cabaña ■ 7791 1094 ■ Open 9am–6pm daily (El Morro); 10am–9pm (San Carlos de la Cabaña) ■ Adm

This vast military complex comprises El Morro castle and the Fortaleza de San Carlos de la Cabaña, the largest fortress in the Americas.

Verdant land surrounding El Morro

Architectural Gems

1 **Edificio Solimar**
MAP V1 ■ Calle Soledad 205, Centro Habana

This remarkable Art Deco apartment complex has curvaceous balconies that wrap around the building.

2 **Catedral de La Habana**
The Baroque facade of this 18th-century church is adorned with pilasters and flanked by asymmetrical bell towers *(see p12)*.

3 **Gran Teatro de La Habana Alicia Alonso**
MAP V5 ■ Paseo de Martí 452 ■ 7861 3076 ■ Open 9am–5pm Mon–Sat, 9am–1pm Sun ■ Adm; extra charge for guided tour

This theater, built in 1837, is a Neo-Baroque confection with corner towers topped by angels. It also features sculptures of the muses Charity, Education, Music, and Theater.

4 **Edificio Bacardí**
MAP W5 ■ Av. Monserrate 261, La Habana Vieja

A stunning example of Art Deco, this soaring, multi-tiered edifice has a facade of pink granite and local limestone. The famous Bacardí bat tops a ziggurat bell tower.

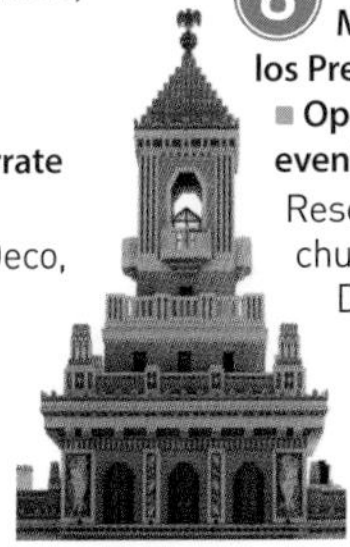

5 **Palacio Presidencial**
MAP W1 ■ Calle Refugio 1

The lavish former presidential palace was intended to signify pomp. It now houses the Museo de la Revolución *(see p75)*. The three-story building is topped by a dome and decorated inside with frescoes and mirrors.

6 **Hotel Habana Libre**
MAP U1 ■ Calle L & 23

Dominating the Vedado skyline, this oblong Modernist tower, built in 1958, features a dramatic atrium lobby, and a huge mural on its exterior by Amelia Peláez *(see p42)*.

The Capitolio's Hall of Lost Steps

7 **Capitolio**
This grandiose congressional building is topped by a dome. Its highlight is the sumptuous Salón de los Pasos Perdidos – the entrance hall, with marble floor and gilded lamps *(see p14)*.

8 **Casa de las Américas**
MAP T1 ■ Calle 3ra & Av. de los Presidentes ■ 7838 2703 ■ Open 10am–4pm Mon–Fri, for events Sat ■ www.casa.cult.cu

Resembling a vertical banded church, this beautiful Art Deco building features a triple-tiered clock tower.

Facade of Edificio Bacardí

9 **Hotel Riviera**
MAP F5 ■ Malecón & Paseo ■ 7836 4051

Overlooking the Malecón, this striking Modernist high-rise was built by mobster boss Meyer Lansky in 1958. Today, it is a National Treasure, with its elegant lobby preserved in exact period detail. The renowned cabaret still functions.

10 **Instituto Superior de Arte**
MAP D2 ■ Calle 120 & 9na, Playa ■ 7208 0704 ■ Open by appointment

Designed by three "rebel" architects, this arts school was never completed, as it was considered too avant-garde.

See map on pp72–3 ←

Music Venues

1 Sábado de la Rumba
MAP S2 ▪ Calle 4 103, Vedado ▪ 7830 3060 ▪ Open 3pm Sat ▪ Adm

Cuba's premier Afro-Cuban dance troupe puts on a great performance and draws people to the dance floor.

2 Palacio de la Rumba
MAP U2 ▪ Calle San Miguel 860, Centro Habana ▪ 7873 0990 ▪ Open from 9pm daily ▪ Adm

Groups such as the kings of rumba, Los Muñequitos de Matanzas, play to a packed house here. Listings are posted in the window of the venue.

3 Café Taberna
MAP X5 ▪ Calle Mercaderes 531, La Habana Vieja ▪ 7861 1637 ▪ Open noon–11pm daily ▪ Adm for shows

Occupying a restored 18th-century mansion, this restaurant has a house band that performs hits from yesteryear.

4 La Bodeguita del Medio
MAP W4 ▪ Calle Empedrado 207, La Habana Vieja ▪ 7801 2637 ▪ Open 10:30am–11:30pm daily

Troubadors play non-stop at this legendary and popular venue, famous for its mojitos and associations with Ernest Hemingway.

5 Tropicana
MAP D2 ▪ Calle 72 & Av. del Ferrocarril, Marianao ▪ 7267 1717 ▪ Open 8:30pm daily ▪ www.cabaret-tropicana.com ▪ Adm for shows

This sensational cabaret, billed as "Paradise Under the Stars," is held in an open-air auditorium, where talented performers in fanciful, ruffled costumes parade under the treetops.

6 Sangri-La
MAP F5 ▪ Calle 42 esq. 21, Miramar ▪ 5264 8343 ▪ Open 6pm–4am daily

One of Havana's sizzling hot private nightclubs, the Sangri-La feels like a piece of Miami in Cuba.

7 La Zorra y El Cuervo
MAP U1 ▪ Ave 23, Vedado ▪ 7833 2402 ▪ Open 10pm–2am ▪ Adm

Top-ranked artists play at what is considered to be Havana's premier jazz club. This compact basement club usually gets crowded.

8 Fabrica de Arte
MAP S2 ▪ Calle 26 esq 11, Vedado ▪ 7838 2260 ▪ Open 8pm–3am Thu–Sun ▪ Adm

This hip multimedia bar, gallery, and event venue has a New York vibe and an ever-changing menu of live performances.

9 Casa de la Música
MAP V2 ▪ Av. Galiano 235, Centro Habana ▪ 7860 8297 ▪ Open 7pm–midnight Fri–Sun ▪ Adm

Hugely popular with Cubans, this is a great place for salsa music. It has excellent afternoon dance matinees.

10 Salón Rojo
MAP U1 ▪ Calle 21 e/ N y O, Vedado ▪ 7833 0666 ▪ Open 10pm–3am Wed–Sun ▪ Adm

Considered to be Havana's top salsa venue, this sizzling red-themed dance club in the upscale Hotel Capri hosts big-name groups, such as Buena Fe and Los Van Van. It is best to arrive after midnight.

Costumed performers at Tropicana

Restaurants

PRICE CATEGORIES

For a three-course meal with half a bottle of wine (or equivalent meal), taxes, and extra charges.

$ under CUP$360 $$ CUP$360–600
$$$ over CUP$600

The nostalgic interior of La Guarida

1 La Guarida

MAP V1 ■ Calle Concordia 418, Centro Habana ■ 7866 9047 ■ $$$

Superb French-inspired cuisine, bohemian ambience, and a one-of-a-kind setting make this a top *paladar [see p126]* in Cuba. Reservations essential.

2 San Cristobal

MAP G5 ■ San Rafael between Campanario and Lealtad, Centro Habana ■ 7860 1705 ■ $$$

Beyoncé and Barack Obama have dined at this antique-filled *paladar* serving delicious *criolla* staples.

3 El Aljibe

MAP F5 ■ Av. 7ma & 24, Miramar ■ 7204 1583 ■ $$

This busy thatched restaurant serves signature all-you-can-eat roast chicken with extras. The well-trained staff are always on their toes.

4 Casa Miglis

MAP V1 ■ Calle Lealtad 120, Centro Habana ■ 5282 7353 ■ $$$

In the renovated ground floor of a rundown townhouse tenement, this offers exciting avant-garde decor and delicious *nouvelle* Cuban cuisine.

5 El Cocinero

MAP T2 ■ Calle 26 between 11 & 13, Vedado ■ 7830 1730 ■ $$$

Housed in a former peanut-oil factory, this elegant restaurant includes an open-air rooftop tapas bar. Food and service are excellent.

6 Coppelia

MAP U1 ■ Calle L & Ave 23, Vedado ■ 7801 1135 ■ $

Lose yourself in the many creamy flavors of Coppelia, touted as the world's largest ice-cream chain. This particular branch has two stories and several open-air parks.

7 La Corte el Principe

MAP F5 ■ Av. 9na & Calle 76, Miramar ■ 5255 9091 ■ $$

Delicious Italian fare prepared and served alfresco by the owner, Sergio. A popular choice is the beef carpaccio.

8 Esquinas Trattoria

MAP W4 ■ Calle Habana 104 esq Cuarteles, Old Havana ■ 7860 6295 ■ $$

A bustling little spot with pavement tables and chairs, Esquinas Trattoria serves delicious pizzas, pastas, and charcuterie platters. Perfect for a pit-stop lunch.

9 Cocina de Lilliam

MAP F5 ■ Calle 48 1311, Miramar ■ 7209 6514 ■ $$

Lilliam, the owner, whips up creative Cuban dishes, such as lobster with pineapple, and ice creams in unusual flavors. You can choose to eat in the air-conditioned interior or in the charming garden with fairy-lights.

10 Jíbaro

MAP X6 ■ Calle Merced 69 e/ Cuba y San Ignacio, Old Havana ■ 7860 1725 ■ $$

Set in a restored colonial mansion, Jíbaro is a great hole-in-the-wall tavern offering lighter versions of Cuban *criolla* food. There's also a fabulous mocktail and cocktail list.

See map on pp72–3

Shopping

1 Centro Cultural Antiguos Almacenes de Depósito San José

MAP X6 ■ Av. Desamparados & San Ignacio, La Habana Vieja ■ Open 9am–6pm Wed–Sun

This handsomely restored waterside warehouse on the edge of the Old City is home to Havana's largest artisan market.

2 Secondhand Book Market

MAP X4 ■ Calle Baratillo, La Habana Vieja

Bibliophiles and bargain-hunters should browse the stalls for books, maps, coins, memorabilia of the Revolution, and curios.

Tienda El Soldadito de Plomo

3 Tienda El Soldadito de Plomo

MAP X5 ■ Calle Muralla 164, La Habana Vieja ■ 7866 0232

An unusual shop where you can buy tiny lead soldiers made on site as well as miniatures of famous characters such as Charlie Chaplin.

4 Dador

MAP W5 ■ Calle Armagura 253 e/Compostela y Habana

A home-grown clothing retailer in a beautiful store off trendy Plaza del Cristo. Three Cuban Habaneras have joined forces to create limited edition contemporary pieces.

5 El Quitrín

MAP X5 ■ Calle Obispo 163, La Habana Vieja ■ 7801 7110

Find hand-embroidered blouses and skirts and traditional *guayabera* shirts.

Taller Experimental de la Gráfica

6 Taller Experimental de la Gráfica

MAP X4 ■ Callejón del Chorro, Plaza de la Catedral, La Habana Vieja ■ 7862 0979

This is the place to buy unique, limited-edition prints hot off the press. You can select from a vast collection of lithographs.

7 Alma

MAP S3 ■ Calle 18 314 e/3ra y 5ta, Miramar ■ 5535 5828 ■ www.almacubashop.com

A beautifully curated store stocking handmade crafts, jewelry, and goods from across Cuba.

8 Clandestina

MAP W2 ■ Calle Villegas between Brasil & Muralla ■ www.clandestina.co

Hip T-shirts by Idania Del Rio and her team of LGBTQ+ designers, plus cool postcards, posters, and prints are on offer here.

9 Casa de la Música EGREM

MAP D2 ■ Calle 20 3309, Miramar ■ 7204 0447 ■ www.egrem.com.cu

EGREM, the state recording company, has the largest selection of music CDs, DVDs, and cassettes in town. Prices, however, are not cheap.

10 Casa del Abanico

MAP W5 ■ Calle Obrapía 107 ■ 7869 7402

Shop here for quality hand-crafted and intricately painted traditional Spanish *abanicos* (fans).

Cigar Venues

1 Casa del Habano Vueltabajera

MAP V5 ■ Hotel Parque Central, Calle Neptuno & Zuleta ■ 7860 6627 ■ Open 9am–6pm daily

Salón Cuaba caters to serious smokers with an elegant smoking lounge and service bar. The staff are knowledgeable.

2 Museo del Tabaco

MAP X5 ■ Calle Mercaderes 120, La Habana Vieja ■ 7861 5795 ■ Open 9:30am–5pm Tue–Sat (to 1pm Sun)

Displaying paraphernalia relating to smoking, this small museum has a cigar shop downstairs.

3 Hostal Conde de Villanueva

MAP X5 ■ Calle Mercaderes 202, La Habana Vieja ■ 7801 1294 ■ Open 10am–7pm

The sumptuous lounge and excellent service make this a great place to sample cigars.

4 Hotel Nacional

You can't really say you have experienced Havana if you haven't settled info a sofa at this hotel's garden terrace bar and smoked a fine cigar, as did Winston Churchill, among other VIPs (see p76).

Tienda de Tabacos Partagás

5 Tienda de Tabacos Partagás

MAP W2 ■ Calle Industria 520, Centro Habana ■ 7862 3772

See fine cigars being rolled in a well-stocked humidor; the shop has a VIP room open by invitation.

6 Fábrica de Tabacos H. Upmann

This factory is a rebranding of the former Romeo y Julieta factory. It offers factory tours and the street-front shop stocks a wide range of cigars in numerous flavors as well as sizes (see p76).

Fábrica de Tabacos H. Upmann

7 Festival del Habano

February ■ www.habanos.com

Attracting celebrities and cigar-lovers, this festival features concerts and a grand finale auction with humidors at the Tropicana cabaret.

8 Club Habana

MAP D2 ■ 5ta Av. 188/192, Playa ■ 7275 0100 ■ Open 9am–7pm Mon–Fri

Within a private members' club, this excellent store and lounge is open to the public via a day pass.

9 Casa del Habano

MAP D2 ■ 5ta Av. & Calle 16, Miramar ■ 7204 7973 ■ Open 10am–7pm daily

A store with a huge humidor stocked with the finest brands. Smoke in comfort in the lounge and bar.

10 Fábrica de Tabacos El Laguito

MAP F5 ■ Av. 146 2302, Cubanacán ■ 7208 0738 ■ By appointment

Aficionados who prefer robust Cohibas, Cuba's flagship brand, may want to buy them at the factory where they're made. The Trinidad label is also hand-rolled here.

See map on pp72–3

ᴛᴏᴘ**10** Western Cuba

Western Cuba is where you'll find some of the loveliest scenery in the country. The dramatic beauty reaches its pinnacle in the Valle de Viñales in Pinar del Río. These mountains are laced with hiking trails, notably at the mountain communities of Soroa and Las Terrazas, and in the Guanahacabibes Peninsula, at the western tip of Cuba. Fine tobacco is grown in fields throughout the Vuelta Abajo region. Just off the mainland is Isla de la Juventud, with an expanse of wild terrain that shelters endemic bird life. Neighboring Cayo Largo, an island in the Archipiélago de los Canarreos, with its white beaches, is a tourist haven.

Hillside orchid garden in Soroa

Cuban orchids

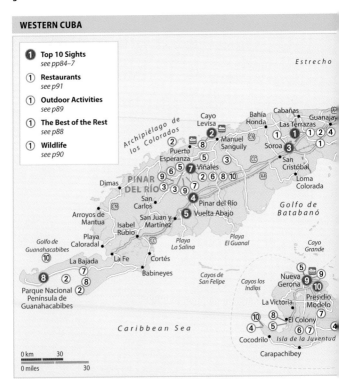

WESTERN CUBA

①	**Top 10 Sights**	*see pp84–7*
①	**Restaurants**	*see p91*
①	**Outdoor Activities**	*see p89*
①	**The Best of the Rest**	*see p88*
①	**Wildlife**	*see p90*

Previous pages Scuba diver in María la Gorda

La Moka focuses on ecotourism and arranges birding and hiking trips. Tourists can walk the well-maintained trails that lead to a coffee plantation and along the San Juan river to cascades and mineral springs. Boats can also be rented on the lake, and there's a zip-line canopy tour.

Lake at Las Terrazas

1 Las Terrazas
MAP C2 ■ Hotel La Moka: Autopista Nacional, km 51, Pinar del Río; 4857 8555 ■ www.lasterrazas.cu

Founded in 1968 as a village in the pine-clad mountains of the eastern Sierra del Rosario, this community *(see p16)* has a lovely setting with simple houses built in terraces overlooking a lake. The local Hotel

2 Cayo Levisa
Ringed by white-sand beaches, this tiny island *(see p54)* off the north coast has a resort hotel and can be reached by ferry from the mainland. A nearby coral reef has splendid crystal-clear dive sites, while the deeper waters farther offshore are populated with marlin and other game fish. The mangroves are also a habitat for waterbirds *(see p53)*.

3 Soroa
MAP C2 ■ Horizontes Villa Soroa: 4852 2910

Surrounded by forested mountains, Soroa, once a center for coffee production, is currently a village offering a scenic escape for nature lovers. Attractions include a stunning orchid garden *(see p16)* displaying more than 700 species. A trail heads sharply downhill to the Cascadas El Salto waterfall, while more challenging hikes lead to the Mirador de Venus – a mountaintop lookout with superlative views. The Hotel & Villas Soroa is a simple, delightful retreat.

Cascadas El Salto waterfall

4 Pinar del Río

MAP B3 ▪ Fábrica de Tabacos Francisco Donatién: 4877 3069; closed for repairs, call to check

Founded in 1669, this is a peaceful town with a sloping main street lined with eclectic buildings, many with Art Nouveau facades. The Palacio de Guasch stands out for its flamboyant exterior. The town is a center of tobacco processing and is home to the Fábrica de Tabacos Francisco Donatién, the local cigar factory.

5 Vuelta Abajo

MAP B3 ▪ Finca El Pinar San Luís, Vegas Robaina ▪ 4879 7470 ▪ Open 9am–5pm Mon–Sat ▪ Adm for guided tours

To the west of the provincial capital, these fertile plains centered on the town of San Juan y Martínez are famed for their tobacco. The leaves, protected from the sun by fine netting, are cured in traditional ranches. The Finca El Pinar Vegas Robaina is a world-famous private tobacco farm well worth a visit.

6 Cayo Largo

MAP F4

Lined with white-sand beaches, Cayo Largo offers horseback riding, sailing, and scuba diving. Excursions whisk you off to nearby isles that are home to flamingos and iguanas. Accommodations range from a marina-side lodge to 4-star all-inclusives (see p127). The island is popular for excursions from Havana and Varadero and for nude sunbathing.

The Viñales church

7 Viñales

MAP B2 ▪ Casa de Don Tomás: Calle Salvador Cisneros 140; 4879 6300 ▪ Casa de la Cultura: Calle José Martí 5; 4877 8128; adm ▪ Centro de Visitantes: 1 mile (1.6 km) SW of Viñales; 4879 6144; open 8am–5pm daily

The agricultural community of Viñales has preserved the colonial architecture of this tiny village. The main street is lined with red-tile-roofed cottages fronted by columned arcades. The Casa de Don Tomás, a replica of the 1822 building destroyed in 2008 by a hurricane, is now a restaurant. A church stands over Parque Martí, where the Casa de la Cultura hosts cultural activities. A visitor center sits atop a *mogote* nearby (see p17).

8 Parque Nacional Península de Guanahacabibes

MAP A3 ▪ Estación Ecológica ▪ 4875 0366 ▪ Adm

Occupying a slender peninsula jutting into the Gulf of Mexico at the western tip of Cuba (see p50), this park – a UNESCO Biosphere Reserve – protects a rare dry forest habitat. Endangered mammals such as the endemic *jutía* and solenodon exist here, as do deer, wild pigs, iguanas, and more than 170 bird species. Guided hikes are offered from the Ecological Station. A paved road runs to Cabo San Antonio, marked by a lighthouse built in 1849; the spot is also good for sportfishing.

Beachside resort at Cayo Largo

9 Nueva Gerona

MAP D4 ■ Iglesia Nuestra Señora de los Dolores: 4632 3361; open hours vary, call to check ■ Museo de Historia Natural: 4632 3143; open 9am–5pm Mon–Sat, 9am–noon Sun

The sleepy capital city of Isla de la Juventud has a graceful colonial core of venerable one-story buildings with columns supporting red-tiled roofs. The Iglesia Nuestra Señora de los Dolores is a lovely church on the main plaza, with a small museum. The Museo de Historia Natural shows re-creations of local natural habitats.

The derelict Presidio Modelo

10 Presidio Modelo

MAP D4 ■ 4632 5112 ■ Open 8am–3pm Mon–Sat, 8am–noon Sun

This former penitentiary *(see p38)* on the outskirts of Nueva Gerona was built in 1926. In October 1953, Fidel Castro and 25 other revolutionaries were imprisoned here after the failed attack on the Moncada barracks *(see p37)*. Today the prison hospital is a museum recalling the 20 months they spent here. Castro's room still contains the collection of books he used to instruct fellow prisoners.

CORK PALM

Found only in a few tiny pockets of the Sierra del Rosario, Cuba's endemic *Palma corcho* is a primitive member of the cycad family. Growing in an ecosystem that is badly threatened by deforestation, the species reproduces with difficulty, although individual palms live to be more than 300 years. As a result, this so-called "living fossil" faces possible extinction.

NORTH COAST DRIVE

▶ **MORNING**

Leave Havana in a rental car and head west along Avenue 5ta, which leads past the Latin American School for Medical Sciences, where international students receive free medical training. Pass through the port town of Mariel, onto Carretera 2-1-3, a winding and gently rolling road frequented by ox-drawn carts. After about two hours of driving past sugarcane fields, turn south at the sign for **Soroa** *(see p85)* and follow the road as it curls uphill through pine forest. Take the time to explore the orchid garden and hike the short trail to the Cascadas El Salto waterfall. Enjoy lunch at one of the restaurants in the area before you go.

AFTERNOON

Returning to the highway, continue west through the towns of Bahía Honda and Las Pozas, with the Sierra del Rosario mountains to the south. The Pan de Guajaibón – a dramatic *mogote* – can be reached by turning south at the hamlet of Rancho Canelo. Farther west beyond Las Pozas, turn north for the ferry dock to **Cayo Levisa** *(see p85)*, where you can enjoy an overnight stay at an island escape. Boats depart twice a day. Alternatively, continue west beyond La Palma to **Viñales**. The road cuts through tobacco fields before emerging in the Valle de San Vicente. Turn southward at the T-junction for Viñales. Two affordable hotels sit atop *mogotes* and *casas particulares* (private rooms) are also available.

See map on pp84–5

The Best of the Rest

1 San Antonio de los Baños
MAP C2

This small colonial town has a museum of humor and echoes with laughter during its biennial Humorismo Gráfico festival.

María la Gorda

2 María la Gorda
MAP A4

This remote and popular dive spot at the far west end of Cuba is set on a gorgeous bay full of coral and other marine life.

3 Cueva de los Portales
A dramatic cavern full of dripstone formations *(see p17)*, which Che Guevara made his headquarters during the Cuban Missile Crisis.

4 Cuevas de Puntas del Este
MAP D4 ▪ c/o Ecotur: Calle 24 & 31, Nueva Gerona; 4632 7101

A permit is required to visit these protected caves adorned with ancient Taíno pictographs.

5 Museo Finca El Abra
MAP D4 ▪ Carretera Siguanea, km 2 ▪ Open 9am–5pm Tue–Sun ▪ Adm

This simple colonial-era farm, where José Martí stayed during his house arrest in 1870, is now a museum.

6 Playa Jibacoa
MAP E2

Jibacoa is a series of beaches popular with Cuban families. Accommodations range from an all-inclusive resort to simple camps popular with Cubans.

7 Criadero de Cocodrilos
MAP D4 ▪ c/o Ecotur: Calle 24 & 31, Nueva Gerona; 4632 7101; ecoturij@enet.cu; guide compulsory

Cuba's endemic crocodile is raised here for reintroduction into the wild. Visit in the early morning to witness feeding time.

8 Reserva Ecológico Los Indios
MAP C4 ▪ c/o Ecotur: Calle 24 & 31, Nueva Gerona; 4632 7101; ecoturij@enet.cu; guide compulsory

These mangroves, grasslands, and forests on the southwest shores of Isla de la Juventud teem with life.

9 Gran Caverna de Santo Tomás
MAP B2 ▪ 20 miles (32 km) west of Viñales ▪ 4868 1274 ▪ Guided tours

In the heart of a *mogote*-studded valley, the Gran Caverna de Santo Tomás *(see p16)* forms the largest underground system in Cuba.

Gran Caverna de Santo Tomás

10 Parque Nacional Punta Francés
MAP C4

At the southwest tip of Isla de la Juventud, stunning coral formations and numerous wrecks make this a superb spot for diving.

Outdoor Activities

Climbing a steep limestone cliff, or mogote, in the Valle de Viñales

① Hiking
Las Terrazas and Soroa *(see p16)* are perfect places for walking, from short strolls to challenging hikes. The two hotels located here can arrange guides *(see p130)*.

② Horseback Riding
Valle del Silencio: 4879 3142
Head for the Mural de la Prehistoria at Valle de Viñales *(see p17)*, or Valle del Silencio, where tobacco farms can be visited.

③ Caving
Sociedad Espeleológica: 4879 6144; presidentesec@cenial.inf.cu
■ **Centro de Visitantes: 4868 1274**
Gran Caverna de Santo Tomás is the place to go to explore Cuba's hidden depths. The Sociedad Espeleológica can arrange visits for serious cavers.

④ Diving
Acclaimed for some of the finest diving in Cuba, La Costa de los Piratas (Pirate Coast) off Punta Francés offers dozens of fantastic dive sites – including the opportunity to explore the wrecks of several sunken Spanish galleons.

⑤ Cycling
The dramatic scenery and peaceful, paved roads of the Valle de Viñales *(see p50)* guarantee cyclists an experience to remember.

⑥ Rock-Climbing
Scaling the *mogotes* of the Valle de Viñales requires skill; more than 100 established climbs have been pioneered by local enthusiasts.

⑦ Bird-Watching
Estación Ecológica, Parque Nacional Guanahacabibes: 4875 0366; guide compulsory
The Guanahacabibes Peninsula is home to more than 170 bird species, including a number of endemics best seen on guided hikes through the La Bajada preserve.

⑧ Swimming
Cayo Levisa: 4875 6501
The crystal-clear waters surrounding Cayo Levisa are ideal for swimming and snorkeling, and the lakes at Las Terrazas *(see p16)* are great for refreshing dips.

⑨ Ziplining
Cubanacán: Calle Salvador Cisneros 63c; 4879 6393; closed for repairs, call to check
Whiz down a single, half-mile- (1-km-) long cable slung between *mogotes* in the Valle de Viñales.

⑩ Fishing
The waters off Cayo Largo offer anglers plenty of thrills, from bone-fish to marlin, which put up a rod-bending struggle to escape.

See map on pp84–5

Wildlife

1 **Mangroves**
Growing at the boundary of land and sea, mangroves form a tangled web of interlocking roots that rise from the waters and provide shelter for juvenile marine creatures. Five species grow in Cuba along both Caribbean and Atlantic shores.

2 **Whale Sharks**
Scuba divers often have close encounters with whale sharks in the warm waters of the Bahía de Corrientes and off Punta Francés.

3 **Turtles**
Female marine turtles crawl onto the shores of pristine Cuban beaches to lay their eggs above the high-water mark. An institute on Cayo Largo specializes in breeding green and hawksbill turtles.

4 **Bone-fish**
This silvery fish is well-camouflaged against the sandy bottoms of shallow lagoons and is notorious for the challenging fight it gives anglers. Cayo Largo is a prime site for bone-fishing.

5 **Spoonbills**
This handsome, rose-colored wading bird has a spatulate bill and is a member of the Ibis family. It nests in among the mangroves and can be seen in the Refugio Ecológico Los Indios (see p88).

6 **Crocodiles**
The swamplands of southern Isla de la Juventud harbor a large population of Cuban crocodiles (see p52). A successful breeding program has brought the species back from the edge of extinction.

7 **Parrots**
Cuba's endemic parrot (see p52) is easily recognized, with its noisy mating calls, red cheeks, white forehead, and blue wing-tips. The dry tropical forests of the Isla de la Juventud have the largest parrot population in Cuba.

Cuban amazon parrots

8 **Marlin**
MAP A4 ▪ María la Gorda: 4875 0118
The fast-flowing Gulf Stream off the north coast of Pinar del Río is a veritable highway for marlin, which give sportfishers a tremendous fight. María la Gorda has a marina and offers sportfishing charters.

9 **Iguanas**
Looking almost lifeless, these giant herbivorous lizards (see p52) crawl around the arid terrain of the Península de Guanahacabibes (see p50) and the infertile Archipiélago de los Canarreos.

10 **Manatees**
These endangered marine mammals inhabit the coastal lagoons off both north and south shores and, although rarely seen, are very common off the Golfo de Guanahacabibes. Manatees feed on seabed grasses and other vegetation.

Cuban crocodile

Restaurants

1 La Fonda de Mercedes
MAP C2 ■ Complejo Las Terrazas, Artemisa ■ c/o 4857 8776 ■ $$

This *paladar* (private restaurant) serves traditional Cuban meals on a terrace overlooking a lake.

2 Casa del Campesino
MAP C2 ■ Complejo Las Terrazas, Artemisa ■ c/o 5225 5516 ■ $

A farmstead where traditional Cuban dishes, cooked in an outdoor oven, are enjoyed under a thatched roof.

3 Restaurante El Cuajaní
MAP B3 ■ Carretera El Moncada, km 2.2, Dos Hermanos ■ 5882 8925 ■ $$

Wonderful, tasty farm-to-fork food served up in a little casita in front of a *mogote* by friendly staff.

4 Eco-Restaurante El Romero
MAP C2 ■ Complejo Las Terrazas, Artemisa ■ c/o 4857 8555 ■ $

Chef Tito presides over a vegetarian paradise, serving delicious and original dishes and juices.

5 Restaurante Las Arcadas
MAP B2 ■ Rancho San Vicente, Carretera a Puerto Esperanza, km 33, Viñales ■ 4879 6201 ■ $$

This hotel restaurant overlooks lush grounds. It serves seafood, pasta, and Cuban staples.

6 Casa de Don Tomás
MAP B2 ■ Calle Salvador Cisneros 147, Viñales ■ 4879 6300 ■ $$

Housed in a historic building, Casa de Don Tomás specializes in *delicias* de Don Tomás, a pork, chicken, and lobster dish, served with rice, beans, and *tostones* (fried plantains). There is traditional live music.

7 3J Tapas
MAP B2 ■ Salvador Cisneros 45, Viñales ■ 4879 3334 ■ $$

Delicious tapas such as stuffed olives, as well as creative *criolla*, international fare and great cocktails are on offer at this lively, contemporary-styled *paladar*.

8 Restaurante Vera
MAP B2 ■ Hotel Los Jazmines, Carretera de Viñales, km 23 ■ 4879 6133 ■ $$

Overlooking the Valle de Viñales from atop a *mogote* (see p17), this location offers the most dramatic view of any restaurant in Cuba.

Scrumptious lobster dish

9 El Galeón
MAP D4 ■ Calle 24 4510, Nueva Gerona ■ 5350 9128 ■ $$

Lots of fabulous seafood plus roast suckling pig dishes are served on a rooftop with live music.

10 El Olivo
MAP B2 ■ Calle Salvador Cisneros 89, Viñales ■ 4869 6654 ■ $$

This private restaurant on the main street of Viñales delivers mouth-watering Italian and Spanish dishes, plus local specials.

See map on pp84–5

🔟 Central Cuba West

Encompassing the provinces of Matanzas, Cienfuegos, and Santa Clara, Central Cuba West is the island's traditional center of tourism. Visitors flock to the white sands of Varadero, and farther east, the Cayos de Villa Clara are fast developing into booming tourist spots. The region is also blessed with wilderness – the Zapata Peninsula shelters Cuban crocodiles and birdlife, while the pine-clad Sierra del Escambray offers mountain trails and waterfalls. History fans are drawn to museums at Playa Girón and Santa Clara. Cienfuegos

is lined with many colonial structures and fin-desiècle mansions, while Matanzas thrums to the rhythms of Afro-Cuban music and dance. At Christmas, the sleepy town of Remedios comes alive with fireworks fever.

Iglesia Virgen del Buen Viaje, Remedios

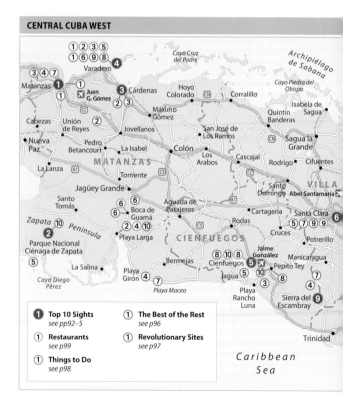

CENTRAL CUBA WEST

① **Top 10 Sights** see pp92–5	① **The Best of the Rest** see p96
① **Restaurants** see p99	① **Revolutionary Sites** see p97
① **Things to Do** see p98	

San Severino Castle, Matanzas

1 Matanzas

MAP E2 ■ Museo Farmacéutico: Plaza de la Libertad; 4524 3179; open 10am–5pm Mon–Sat; 10am–2pm Sun; adm ■ Castillo de San Severino: Zona Industrial; 4528 3259; open 9am–4pm Tue–Sat, 9am–noon Sun; adm

This historic port town, which evolved as a trading center for sugar and enslaved people, was dubbed the "Athens of Cuba" when artistic life flourished here during the 19th century. Plaza de la Libertad and Plaza de la Vigía are home to the Catedral de San Carlos and Museo Farmacéutico. Visit San Severino castle's slave-trade museum and, outside town, Cuevas de Bellamar's caverns.

2 Parque Nacional Ciénaga de Zapata

MAP E3 ■ National Park Office: Playa Larga; 4598 7248; open 8am–4:30pm daily; adm includes a guide

This vast park is the most complete wildlife preserve in Cuba. Swamps cover the region, while mangroves, reeds, and wet forests also provide varied habitats that support more than 200 bird species, such as the Cuban pygmy owl and the tiny *zunzuncito (see p53)*. Manatees swim in coastal lagoons, Cuban crocodiles lurk inland, and flamingos flock to Laguna de las Salinas. Official guides lead nature-oriented tours, and most local inhabitants now make a living by renting rooms or acting as guides for tourists.

Museo Oscar María de Rojas, Cárdenas

3 Cárdenas

MAP F2

The workaday port town of Cárdenas offers some intriguing attractions. A good starting point is tiny Parque Colón, where a statue of Christopher Columbus stands in front of the 1826 Catedral de la Concepción Inmaculada. The Museo Oscar María de Rojas *(see p46)* has fascinating displays with some artifacts dating back to pre-Columbian days. Horse-drawn taxi-cabs traverse town.

Luxury hotels line the beach at Varadero

4 Varadero
MAP F2

The beach here, at Cuba's top resort, offers plenty of watersports, but shade is in short supply. Away from the beach, regional attractions include hiking and scuba diving. Golfers are also catered for at the 18-hole course at Mansión Xanadú (see p131). Most hotels in the area are large, all-inclusive resorts, but visitors can also choose from a handful of smaller options.

Palacio del Valle, Cienfuegos

5 Cienfuegos
MAP G3

Set along a bay, Cienfuegos was founded in 1819, when French settlers laid out a grid around the Plaza de Armas, now Plaza Martí. The Paseo del Prado slopes down to the Punta Gorda district, where Art Nouveau and mid-20th-century Modernist homes can be rented. A highlight of any visit is a meal at Palacio del Valle, a mansion decorated in Moorish fashion (see p99).

6 Santa Clara
MAP H3 ■ Teatro de la Caridad, Parque Vidal 3: 4520 5548; open 9am–4pm Mon–Sat; adm

Known as the "city of the heroic guerrilla," Santa Clara is an industrial and university town from where, in 1958, Che Guevara led the final battle to topple Batista (see p37). Visitors flock to sites associated with the battle, such as the Tren Blindado (a derailed armored train) and the Complejo Escultórico Ernesto Che Guevara (see p97). Also of interest is the frescoed ceiling of the Teatro de la Caridad (Charity Theater).

7 Cayos de Villa Clara
MAP J1

These islands lie 45 miles (72 km) from the mainland, to which they are connected by a very narrow *pedraplén* (causeway). The calm peacock-blue sea is protected by a coral reef and is ideal for swimming and snorkeling – the deeper waters beyond the reef offer diving. Catamaran and sportfishing excursions depart from a marina.

MANJUARÍ

The manjuarí, a primitive fish from the ante-diluvian dawn evolved at least 270 million years ago, about the time the first reptiles crawled out of the seas. Growing to 6 ft (2 m) long, it has an elongated snout like a crocodile's and scaly skin covered with natural oil. Endemic to Cuba, this dark green fish inhabits the Zapata swamps.

8 Remedios

MAP H3 ■ Museo de la Música Alejandro García Caturla: 4239 6851; open 9am–noon, 1–5pm Tue–Sat, 9am–noon Sun ■ Museo de las Parrandas: open 1:30–4pm Mon, 9am–noon Sun

Founded in 1513, this is a quiet, colonial-era city with a church famed for its gilded altar. The Museo de la Música Alejandro García Caturla displays musical instruments, while the Museo de las Parrandas exhibits objects linked to the city's famous Christmas Eve festival (see p69).

Colonnaded buildings in Remedios

9 Sierra del Escambray
MAP H3

Spanning three provinces, this rugged mountain range rises inland from the Caribbean coast, reaching 3,790 ft (1,155 m) atop Pico San Juan. Coffee is farmed on the lower slopes, while the densely forested upper slopes are of great ecological value for their plants and profuse birdlife. Topes de Collantes (see p51) offers accommodation and is a base for guided nature hikes.

10 Caibarién
MAP H3

A once-important port town that still lives partly off its humble fishing fleet, sprawling Caibarién has a dishevelled countenance and awaits a renaissance of its incredible wealth of architecture, with buildings from Neo-Classical to Art Nouveau centered on Parque de la Libertad. The town also has beaches, and mangroves teeming with birds.

JAGÜEY GRANDE TO CIENFUEGOS DRIVE

▶ MORNING

Start your day early with a visit to **Central Australia** (see p19). After a brief tour, including a possible steam-train ride, drive south along the ruler-straight road with the grassy swamps of **Zapata** (see pp18–19) on each side. Stop off at La Boca de Guamá to see the **crocodile breeding farm** (see p18) and then at Centro Ecológico, where an ecological trail lets you experience the Zapata ecosystems firsthand. At **Playa Larga** (see p97), follow the main road south along the shoreline toward Playa Girón. Take time to browse the Bay of Pigs exhibits and displays (see p37) at the fascinating **Museo Girón** (see p19) then continue 5 miles (8 km) east to **Caleta Buena** (see p19). Enjoy lunch and an hour or two snorkeling in this sheltered cove. Note that in March and April, the road is smothered with crabs migrating inland to spawn. They are a hazard; ensure that your tires have plenty of tread to reduce the chance of getting a puncture from broken shells.

AFTERNOON

Retrace your path to Playa Girón and turn north; the route is potholed in places. At Bermejas, turn right. Observe daily rural Cuban life in the remote settlements you pass through. Turn right onto Carretera 3-1-2, the main highway that leads to the well-planned maritime city of **Cienfuegos**. Spend the rest of the day admiring its Neo-Classical structures, ending with a seafood meal at the **Palacio del Valle** (see p99).

See map on pp92–3 ←

The Best of the Rest

1 Cuevas de Bellamar
MAP E2 ▪ Carretera de las Cuevas de Bellamar ▪ 4526 1683 ▪ Open 9am–5pm Tue–Sun ▪ Adm ▪ Several tours daily

This extensive cave system has fascinating dripstone features. A small museum located here details the geological processes.

2 San Miguel de los Baños
This atmospheric town is set amid the rolling hills of Matanzas. Find many elaborate Neo-Classical and Beaux Arts mansions and clapboard bungalows here.

3 Laguna Guanaroca
MAP G3

Flamingos stalk the water at this protected lagoon, a favorite spot for water birds. Visit early to see the wildlife.

4 El Nicho
MAP G3 ▪ 32 miles (52 km) east of Cienfuegos ▪ 4254 0117 ▪ Open 8am–6pm daily ▪ Adm

Cuba's most beautiful waterfall plummets down the north side of the Sierra Escambray into cool, turquoise pools.

Cannons at Castillo de Jagua

5 Castillo de Jagua
MAP G3 ▪ Poblado Castillo de Jagua ▪ 4359 6402 ▪ Open 9am–5pm Mon–Sat, 9am–1pm Sun ▪ Adm

This tiny fortress guarding the entrance to Cienfuegos Bay still has a working drawbridge across the moat.

The lagoon at Boca de Guamá

6 Boca de Guamá
MAP F3 ▪ 4591 5662

Beside Laguna del Tesoro, this hotel complex offers one-hour boat tours of the lagoon.

7 Lago Hanabanilla
MAP H3 ▪ Hotel Hanabanilla: 4220 1100

This reservoir is on the Sierra del Escambray's northern slopes. The no-frills Hotel Hanabanilla stands over the western shore.

8 Pepito Tey
MAP G3

The sugar mill town of Pepito Tey, preserves the rambling plantation home of Edwin F. Atkins, Cuba's largest plantation owner at the turn of the 21st century and founder of the botanical gardens on the opposite side. The home is now a museum.

9 Museo de Agroindustria Azucarero Marcelo Salado
MAP H3 ▪ 4236 3586 ▪ Open 9am–4pm Mon–Fri, alternate Sat ▪ Adm

Learn about the history of Cuba's sugar industry and hop aboard for a ride on one of this museum's antique steam trains.

10 Jardín Botánico Soledad
MAP G3 ▪ Pepito Tey ▪ (43) 54 5115 ▪ Open 8am–4pm ▪ Adm

A botanical garden houses one of the world's largest palm collections, and other plants.

See map on pp92–3

Revolution Sites

1 Castillo El Morrillo

MAP F2 ■ Canímar, Matanzas ■ Open 8am–4pm daily ■ Adm

This fortress houses the mausoleum of two martyred revolutionary leaders: Antonio Guiteras Holmes and Carlos Aponte Hernández.

2 Museo de la Batalla de Ideas

MAP F2 ■ Av. 6 between 11 & 12, Cárdenas: 4552 3990 ■ Open 9am–5pm Tue–Sat, 9am–1pm Sun ■ Adm

A museum recounting the custody battle over Elián González, a Cuban boy rescued from sea off Miami.

3 Museo Casa Natal de José Antonio Echeverría

MAP F2 ■ Genes between Calzada & Coronel Verdugo, Cárdenas ■ 4552 4145 ■ Open 9am–4:30pm Tue–Sat, 9am–1:30pm Sun ■ Adm

This museum was once the home of José Antonio Echeverría (see p41).

4 Museo Girón

The Bay of Pigs invasion is recounted at this museum with armaments and maps (see p19).

5 Tren Blindado

MAP H3 ■ Av. Independencia between Línea & Puente de la Cruz, Santa Clara ■ 4220 2758 ■ Open 9am–5pm Mon–Fri, 9am–noon Sat–Sat ■ Adm

This monument re-creates the derailing of an armored train by Che's guerrillas using the original carriages.

6 Central Australia

This site preserves the building that was Castro's headquarters during the Bay of Pigs (see p19).

7 Complejo Escultórico Ernesto Che Guevara

MAP H3 ■ Plaza de la Revolución, Santa Clara ■ 4220 5668 ■ Museum & Memorial: open 9am–4:30pm Tue–Sun

A statue of Che looms over this site, which features a museum and Che's mausoleum (see p39).

8 Museo Naval

MAP G3 ■ Calle 21 & Av. 62, Cienfuegos ■ 4351 6617 ■ Open 10am–6pm Tue–Sat, 9am–1pm Sun ■ Adm

The site of an anti-Batista revolt on September 5, 1957, this former naval headquarters is now a museum.

9 Museo Provincial Abel Santamaría

MAP H3 ■ Calle Esquerra, Santa Clara ■ 4220 3041 ■ Closed for repairs, call to check ■ Adm

A small museum dedicated to the revolutionary movement in Santa Clara is housed in this former military barracks.

10 Playa Larga

MAP F3

On April 17, 1961, CIA-sponsored Cuban exiles landed on this beach in the Bay of Pigs (see p37).

Tren Blindado

Things to Do

Boats off the beach at Varadero

1 Sailing
Small sailing boats can be rented at Rancho Luna and Varadero *(see p94)*, from where boat trips to outlying cays depart and tropical cocktails are served as the sun sets.

2 Scuba Diving
Diving enthusiasts will enjoy the region's north and south shores. Playa Larga *(see p97)* is famed for its coral reefs, and Varadero is popular for its sunken warships.

3 Learning to Dance
Matanzas *(see p93)* is an excellent venue for learning to dance like a Cuban. Festivals that take place in October and November feature dance workshops.

4 Boat Tour
Tour the Bay of Cienfuegos on a boat exploring its islands and visit the Castillo de Jagua. Book with Marina Cienfuegos.

5 Angling for Bone-Fish
The region offers some of the best bone-fishing in the Caribbean. The shallow lagoons off southern Zapata *(see p93)* and Cayos de Villa Clara *(see p94)* are the best spots. Hotels offer guided fishing trips.

6 Horse-Carriage Tour
Formal excursions by colonial-era, horse-drawn carriages are a popular way to explore Varadero and Cienfuegos *(see p94)*, while in all other cities you can hop aboard one of the rickety *coches* that ply the main streets as slow-moving taxis for locals.

7 Snorkeling at Caleta Buena
MAP F3
The whole region is very good for snorkeling, but this cove *(see p19)* near Playa Girón offers a display of corals, sponges, and tropical fish. Snorkeling gear is available for rent. Lunch and snacks are served during the course of the day.

8 Paragliding
Varadero is the place for this thrilling activity, where you strap on a harness attached to a giant kite pulled by a speedboat. In seconds you're soaring, with a bird's view of the beach resort far below.

9 Golf
MAP F2 ■ Av. Las Américas, km 8.5 ■ 4566 7788 ■ www.varaderogolfclub.com
The Varadero Golf Club, at Mansion Xanadú, is Cuba's only 18-hole golf course, although more are planned. Laid out along the shore, it offers a demanding breeze-swept challenge between the sands and a lagoon.

Cuban emerald hummingbird

10 Birding
Parque National Ciénaga de Zapata and the Sierra del Escambray teem with many bird species. Look for parrots and hummingbirds, and flamingos in the lagoons *(see p52)*.

Restaurants

PRICE CATEGORIES
For a three-course meal with half a bottle of wine (or equivalent meal), taxes and extra charges.
....
$ under CUP$360 $$ CUP$360–600
$$$ over CUP$600

1 El Mesón del Quijote
MAP F2 ■ Av. Las Américas, Varadero ■ $$

Perched on top of a grassy hill, this restaurant re-creates the mood of a Spanish *bodega* with its rustic decor.

2 Varadero 60
MAP F2 ■ Av. 60 & Calle 60, Varadero ■ 5572 1414 ■ $$

Housed in a converted mansion, this restaurant sporting 1950s decor serves wood-fired dishes such as shrimp with brandy.

3 Salsa Suárez
MAP F2 ■ Calle 31 103, Varadero ■ 4561 4194 ■ $$$

This classy, private restaurant has a charming and sophisticated nautical-themed dining room. Try the seafood cannelloni.

4 Chuchi el Pescador
MAP F3 ■ Caletón, Bahia de los Cochinos ■ 4598 7336 ■ $$

A popular long-standing restaurant serving fresh seafood and other Cuban staples. Just a short hop from the village of Caletón.

5 Restaurante La Fondue
MAP F2 ■ Av. 1ra & Calle 62, Varadero ■ 4563 1039 ■ $$

Imported cheeses find their way into creative fondues, but squid in tomato sauce is also on the menu.

6 Tiki
MAP F3 ■ Bahía de Cochinos ■ 4598 7285 ■ $$

This open-air *paladar* under thatch has great views over the Bay of Pigs and serves tasty seafood and *criolla* dishes.

7 Le Fettucine
MAP E2 ■ Calle Milanés 29018 e/ Zaragoza and Santa Teresa ■ 5412 2553 ■ $$

This small restaurant offers delicious, homemade pasta.

8 Palacio del Valle
MAP G3 ■ Calle 37 & Av. 0, Cienfuegos ■ 4366 1445 ■ $$

The surroundings astound in this grandiose mansion in Moorish style, with spectacular views of the bay. The rooftop bar is perfect for a sunset cocktail. Musicians entertain guests in the evenings.

The lavish interior of Palacio del Valle

9 Paladar Hostal Florida Center
MAP H3 ■ Calle Maestra Nicolasa 56, Santa Clara ■ 4220 8161 ■ $

Dine on the flower-filled patio of this beautiful 19th-century colonial home. Host Angel cooks and serves delicious food, such as shrimp in tomato sauce, to the accompaniment of Cuban tunes. Book ahead.

10 Finca del Mar
MAP G3 ■ Calle 35 between 18 & 20, Cienfuegos ■ 4366 1706 ■ $$

This class act is the best private restaurant in town. Owner Omar is in charge of delicious *nouvelle* and traditional dishes. There is also a delightful outdoor dining terrace with bay views and music videos.

See map on pp92–3

⏹10 Central Cuba East

From the atmospheric city of Trinidad to the gorgeous beaches of the Jardines del Rey, this region is one of the most exciting in Cuba. The terrain ranges from the former sugar territory of the Valle de los Ingenios and the forested mountains around Topes de Collantes to the tourist-friendly white-sand spots in Cayo Coco, Guillermo, and Cruz. Trinidad, one of Cuba's most vibrant cities, is a wonderful base for exploring Topes and for scuba diving off the beach at nearby Playa Ancón. Camagüey is noted for its colonial architecture. The Carretera Central connects the key sites, but the pristine maritime wilderness of Jardines de la Reina is accessible solely by boat.

Sancti Spiritus church

CENTRAL CUBA EAST

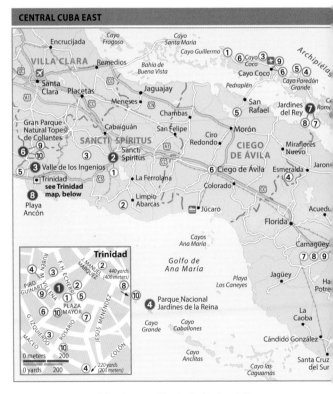

Previous pages *A beautiful beach at one of the islands of Jardines del Ray*

Musicians in Trinidad

1 Trinidad

Cuba's most endearing city was founded in 1514 by Diego Velázquez and named a UNESCO World Heritage Site in 1988. Closed to traffic, the cobbled streets have remained largely unchanged since the 18th century, when Trinidad grew wealthy from trade in slavery and sugar. The museums, churches, and plazas are intriguing, but the real joy is in wandering the narrow streets and observing daily life *(see pp20–21)*.

2 Sancti Spíritus

MAP J3 ▪ Iglesia Parroquial Mayor del Espíritu Santo: Calle Agramonte Oeste 58, 4132 4855; open 9–11am & 2–5pm Tue–Sun; adm

Founded in 1522, this city is often overlooked by visitors, who tend to focus on neighboring Trinidad. The historic core of Sancti Spíritus has elegant mansions and brightly colored colonial homes graced by wrought-iron lanterns and grills. Sights include the Yayabo bridge and Parque Serafín Sánchez. The highlight is Plaza Honorato, with its Casa de la Trova and the lovely Iglesia Parroquial Mayor del Espíritu Santo – a 17th-century church with a spectacular ceiling.

Valle de los Ingenios

3 Valle de los Ingenios

MAP H4 ▪ Hacienda Manaca Iznaga: Iznaga; 4199 7241; adm

Northeast of Trinidad, this area gets its name from the many *ingenios* (sugar mills) built during the 18th and 19th centuries, when vast sugar plantations occupied the entire valley. While many of the sugarcane estates have been restored as museums and hostels, the main house of the Manaca Iznaga estate has been converted into a restaurant. Climb its 147-ft (45-m) tower for a great view of the valley. At the foot of the tower, local women set up stalls to sell traditional lacework.

Camagüey

Bahía de Gloria *Cayo Guajaba*

Cayo Sabinal ② Playa Santa Lucía ⑨

enado Nuevitas

Minas

CAMAGÜEY Santa Lucía

Ignacio Agramonte

Sibanicú ● Manatí

Palo Seco Vázquez

Najasa

① ⑧ Guáimaro

Jobabo ⑩ Las Tunas

LAS TUNAS

Amancio

Guayabal Playa Habanero

0 km 25

0 miles 25

Parque Nacional Jardines de la Reina

④ Parque Nacional Jardines de la Reina

MAP J4 ■ Avalon Dive Center; www.cubandivingcenters.com

Over 600 deserted isles scattered off the Ciego de Ávila and Camagüey provinces form an oceanic Eden populated by sharks and Goliath Groupers, and protected by a long coral reef. Marine turtles lay their eggs on beaches, while iguanas laze in the sun and flamingos wade in the shallows. Four cruise vessels and a floating hotel cater to anglers and divers.

⑤ Camagüey

The plazas of the third-largest city in Cuba are lined with colonial and Neo-Classical buildings. The city's network of streets – designed to thwart pirates – can be confusing to visitors. Sites include the Catedral, museums, and the Teatro Principal – home to the Ballet de Camagüey. The best of the city's nightlife can be experienced at the Casa de la Trova on Plaza Agramonte (see pp26–7).

⑥ Gran Parque Natural Topes de Collantes

MAP H4 ■ Gaviota Topes de Collantes: 4254 0231

The steep drive to the northwest of Trinidad is well rewarded at Topes de Collantes, which functions as a base for hikes to the Caburní waterfall and the colonial-era coffee estate at Finca Codina, where caves and a beautiful orchid garden can be explored. Topes has some hotels in its vicinity, plus a tourist information center, and Gaviota, which oversees the complex, organizes tours and guides, including excursions from nearby Trinidad.

⑦ Jardines del Rey

Off the north coast of Ciego de Ávila and Camagüey, the Jardines del Rey (King's Gardens) archipelago comprises about 400 islands, mostly uninhabited. Cayo Coco, one of the largest isles, and neighboring Cayo Guillermo and Cayo Cruz have tourist hotels and watersports along their beaches. The diving is good here, and flamingos flock to the inshore lagoons (see pp24–5).

⑧ Playa Ancón

MAP H4

The slender Península de Ancón south of Trinidad is lined by a fine, white-sand beach (see p20) served by three tourist hotels. With shallow waters good for swimming and snorkeling, it is also frequented by

Camagüey's colorful city center

LA TROCHA

A line of defence was built by the Spanish during the 19th-century Wars of Independence to block the advance of Cuban nationalist forces, the *mambises*. La Trocha stretched across Cuba from Morón, north of Ciego de Ávila, to Júcaro, on the Caribbean coast, and featured fortified towers.

the locals. A dive center arranges trips to Cayo Blanco to view the fabulous black coral formations. A marina rents out sailboats to visitors prior to their arrival in Cuba.

Secluded Playa Santa Lucía

⑨ Playa Santa Lucía
MAP M3

This isolated resort has a lovely beach and fantastic opportunities for diving and seeing bull sharks being hand fed. Horse-drawn carriages visit nearby Playa Los Cocos, an even lovelier beach adjoining a ramshackle fishing village. Most dining is limited to all-inclusive hotels, a handful of casas, and private restaurants.

⑩ Las Tunas
MAP M4 ▪ Museo Histórico Provincial: Calle Francisco Varona and Colón; 3134 8201; open 9am–5pm Tue–Thu, 1–9pm Fri–Sat, 8am–noon Sun; adm

Located between central and eastern Cuba, Las Tunas suffered during the Wars of Independence (see p36), when it was razed by fire. Carretera Central runs through the heart of the city and is lined with charming houses. The main square features a museum of provincial history, and the local tradition of ceramic art thrives here.

A DAY IN CAMAGÜEY

▶ **MORNING**

A day is barely enough to explore this historically significant town. Get an early start in the morning in **Parque Agramonte** (see p27) to see the cathedral and Casa de la Trova. Exit the square by following Calle Cisneros south. After two blocks, turn right. The street brings you to **Plaza San Juan de Dios** (see p26), surrounded by 18th-century houses. Explore the museum inside the Iglesia y Hospital San Juan de Dios, then follow Calle Matias west three blocks. Turn right onto Calle 24 de Febrero. After five blocks, cobbled **Plaza del Carmen** (see p26) opens to the northwest at the junction with Calle Martí, and has life-like sculptures scattered about. Lunch on *boliche mechado* at **La Campaña de Toledo** (see p109).

AFTERNOON

Retrace your steps to Calle Martí and follow it east to Parque Agramonte. Turn left onto Calle Cisneros to reach Plaza de los Trabajadores. On your right, **Casa Natal Ignacio Agramonte** (see p26) is worth a peek before exploring the **Catedral Nuestra Señora de la Merced** (see p26). Don't miss its silver sepulchre. Exit the square to the northwest and walk one block to the **Teatro Principal** (see p27) on your right. Then head north along Calle Enrique José to the **Museo Ignacio Agramonte** (see p27). Continue south along Calle República to return to the center.

See map on pp102–3

Colonial Trinidad

1 Plaza Mayor
Trinidad's main square is surrounded by 18th-century mansions. Two bronze greyhounds on the south side are popular with kids (see p20).

Convento de San Francisco de Asís

2 Convento de San Francisco de Asís
MAP Y1 ■ Calle Hernández Echerri 59 & Guinart ■ 4199 4121 ■ Open 9am–5pm daily ■ Adm
Built in 1730 by Franciscan monks, this convent is currently home to the Museo de la Lucha Contra Bandidos.

3 Palacio Brunet
With marble floors, decorative tilework, and fan windows, this mansion is now the Museo Romántico, featuring period furniture (see p20).

4 Plazuela de Jigüe
MAP Y1
This plaza was named after the *jigüe* (acacia) tree beneath which Father Bartolomé de las Casas celebrated the city's first mass in 1514.

5 Iglesia Parroquial de la Santísima Trinidad
MAP Z1 ■ Plaza Mayor ■ Open 11am–12:30pm Mon–Sat
The Church of the Holy Trinity was built in 1892 on the site of the original parish church and has a Gothic altar.

6 Palacio Cantero
Home to the Museo Histórico, this gem is filled with sumptuous period furnishings and exhibits on Trinidad's history (see p21).

7 Museo de Arquitectura Colonial
This exquisite museum has excellent displays showing the evolution of architectural styles specific to Trinidad (see p46).

8 Iglesia de Santa Ana
MAP J3 ■ Calle Camilo Cienfuegos & Calle José Mendoza
At the northeast corner of the old city, this semi-derelict 18th-century church stands over a small plaza. There's also a lively cultural center located in a former prison.

9 Casa Templo de Santería Yemayá
MAP Y1 ■ Rubén Martínez Villena 59
Learn about the lores of Santería, the syncretic Afro-Cuban religion, at Casa Templo. This colonial home of a practitioner has an altar dedicated to Yemayá, the Virgin of Regla.

Casa Templo de Santería Yemayá

10 Plaza de Tres Cruces
MAP Y1 ■ Calle Rubén Martínez Villena & Isidro Armenteros
This spacious plaza surrounded by simple homes is pinned by three wooden crosses. For centuries, it has been the terminus for the annual Vía de las Cruces Easter Procession.

See map on pp102–3

The Cays

(1) Cayo Guillermo
Linked to Cayo Coco by a narrow causeway, this lovely little cay is blessed with warm waters and stunning beaches. Its bountiful mangroves provide good opportunities for those interested in bird-watching (see p24).

Scuba diver filming sharks in Jardines de la Reina

(2) Cayo Sabinal
A remote cay that is accessible solely by a rough dirt road or by boat excursions from Playa Santa Lucía, Cayo Sabinal has three spectacular beaches, but facilities are scarce. Wild pigs roam the scrub-covered interior (see p25).

(3) Cayo Coco
MAP K2
More than 14 miles (23 km) of gorgeous white beaches, crystal-clear turquoise ocean, lagoons, coral reefs, and excellent all-inclusive hotels draw visitors from far and wide to Cayo Coco.

(4) Cayo Cruz
A new pedraplén opens up Cayo Cruz, developed with three hotels along 16 miles (25 km) of pristine white sand shelving into shallow turquoise water.

(5) Cayo Paredón Grande
MAP L2
This scrub-covered cay offers a beach with a superb bar. Watersports can also be arranged through your hotel. Built in 1859, the intriguing Faro Diego Velázquez lighthouse is located here.

Faro Diego Velázquez lighthouse

(6) Diving with Sharks
Certified divers can experience thrilling encounters with sharks on organized dives at Cayo Coco and Playa Santa Lucía. Whale sharks may be spotted at Jardines de la Reina.

(7) Cayo Romano
MAP L2
Spectacular coral reefs await visitors to this large uninhabited cay. A road connects to the mainland at Brasil and east from Cayo Coco.

(8) Fishing
Enthusiasts of fishing can follow the example of Ernest Hemingway who trawled the clear waters off the Jardines del Rey (see p104) for marlin and other game fish. Sportfishing trips are offered from the resorts.

(9) Centro de Investigaciones de Ecosistemas Costeros
MAP K2 ▪ Cayo Coco ▪ 3330 1161
This research center for the study and protection of coastal and marine ecosystems is open to the public and features exhibits on manatees, flamingos, and coral reefs.

(10) Hotel Flotante La Tortuga
MAP K4
In the heart of the Jardines de la Reina, this floating hotel plays host to diving and fishing excursions. The only hotel in the cays, it is anchored within a protected lagoon.

Landscape Features

1 Mogotes
MAP M4

These dramatic limestone forms *(see p17)* add beauty to the pleasure of hiking in the Área Protegida de Recursos Manejados Sierra del Chorrillo, southeast of Camagüey.

2 Sugarcane Fields
The southern half of the Sancti Spíritus province is a veritable sea of sugarcane, extending east into much of Ciego de Ávila province. Feathery fronds rise from the stalks during the dry summer months.

3 Rugged Mountains
MAP J3 ▪ La Sabina: Carretera Cacahual; 4155 4930; ecoturss@enet.cu

The craggy, thickly forested Alturas de Banao formed a base for Che Guevara's guerrilla army in 1958. Trails lead out from La Sabina, an ecological study camp offering accommodation in rooms and tents.

4 Coral Cays
Enhanced by their setting in seas of jade and aquamarine, coral cays speckle the oceans off Central Cuba East. Most are uninhabited but offer excellent wildlife viewing.

5 Plains
Hardy cattle munch the windswept, grassy savannah plains of the eastern Ciego de Ávila and Camagüey provinces, where the *vaquero* (cowboy) lifestyle is still very much alive.

6 Lakes
MAP K2 ▪ Morón

Anglers delight in the many fish species near Sancti Spíritus, and in the milky-colored Laguna de la Leche and Lago de Redonda, both outside Morón.

7 Beaches
Sandy beaches unfurl along the Atlantic shore of the Jardines del Rey *(see pp24–5)*. The stunning cays of the Jardines de la Reina *(see p104)* are also ringed by pearly white sands. The mainland shore has few splendid beaches *(see pp54–5)*.

8 Tropical Forest
MAP L4

Dense montane forests cloak much of this region. Sierra del Chorrillo, south of Camagüey, is an excellent venue for those who want to explore the tropical dry forests.

9 Underground Caves
Caves make up a large part of the limestone uplands around Topes de Collantes *(see p51)*. The Cueva del Jabalí at Cayo Coco *(see p107)* features a restaurant and cabaret.

10 Waterfalls
Drenched in rainfall, the Sierra del Escambray around Topes de Collantes *(see p51)* resounds to the thunderous noise of cascades splashing into crystal-clear pools. The Salto de Caburní is easily reached by a well-trodden trail.

Colorful coral reef

Restaurants

1 Mesón de la Plaza

MAP J3 ■ Calle Máximo Gómez 34, Sancti Spíritus ■ 4132 8546 ■ $$

Re-creating the rustic ambience of a Spanish *bodega* with cowhide chairs and benches, this restaurant serves bargain-priced dishes.

Mesón de la Plaza

2 Gourmet Restaurant

MAP H4 ■ Calle José Martí 262, Trinidad ■ 4199 6070 ■ $$$

A plush option within the Iberostar Gran Hotel Trinidad. International dishes are prepared with aplomb.

3 Muñoz Tapas Calle Gutiérrez

MAP Y2 ■ Corner of Calle Desengño ■ 4199 3673 ■ www.munoztapas.com ■ $$

Family-run Spanish and Cuban tapas spot on a rooftop terrace. Great cocktails.

4 Guitarra Mía

MAP H4 ■ Calle Jesus Menéndez 19 between Cienfuegos & Pérez, Trinidad ■ 4199 3452 ■ $$

This homely restaurant serves delicious *criollo* dishes to the accompaniment of live music. The owner is a famous guitarist.

5 Restaurante Manacas Iznaga

MAP H4 ■ Iznaga, Valle de los Ingenios ■ 4199 7241 ■ $$

This former sugar-estate owner's mansion provides a unique setting for enjoying traditional Cuban dishes.

6 Blanco y Negro

MAP K3 ■ Calle Independencia 388, Ciego de Ávila ■ 3320 7744 ■ Open noon–11pm daily ■ $

Dine on fried chicken, paella, or *ropa vieja* (shredded beef with vegetables), all well executed by the owner-chef. The *trio de carnes* house special is also a bargain.

7 Restaurante 1800

MAP L3 ■ Plaza San Juan de Dios, Camagüey ■ 3228 3619 ■ $$

This elegant private restaurant offers period furnishings, a great location, and an excellent buffet (menu options are also available). There are tables on the cobbled plaza outside.

8 Gran Hotel by Melia

MAP L3 ■ Calle Maceo 64, Camagüey ■ 3229 2314 ■ $$

The Gran Hotel's rooftop restaurant offers a quality buffet dinner. The fine views over the city center are a definite bonus.

9 La Campaña de Toledo

MAP L3 ■ Plaza San Juan de Dios, Camagüey ■ 3228 6812 ■ $$

Located in the center of Camagüey, opposite one of the most emblematic plazas in the town, La Campaña de Toledo's signature dish is *boliche mechado*, a local beef delicacy.

10 Adita Café

MAP H4 ■ Calle Maceo 452B esq Calle Gutierrez ■ www.aditacafe.com ■ $$

Centrally located restaurant serving good all-day Cuban and international dishes. It's a sister spot to popular Restaurant San José.

See map on pp102–3

🔟 The Far East

Far-eastern Cuba is dominated by rugged mountains. The Sierra Maestra was the major base of Fidel Castro's guerrilla army *(see p40)*. Sierra Cristal and Sierra Purial are a wilderness of mountain rainforest and offer spectacular hiking and birding. The coastline is no less rugged, with lovely beaches lining the shore of Holguín. Historic cities dot this corner of the republic. Santiago de Cuba *(see pp30–31)* – birthplace of the Revolution – teems with sites of cultural note, while Baracoa is the country's oldest city. Cuba's African heritage is keenly felt in Santiago de Cuba and Guantánamo.

The palm-studded Playa Guardalavaca, Holguín

THE FAR EAST

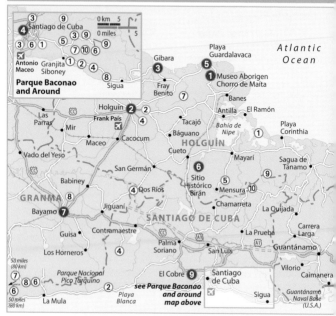

① Museo Aborigen Chorro de Maíta

MAP P4 ■ 5 miles (8 km) east of Guardalavaca ■ 2443 0201 ■ Open 9am–5pm Mon–Sat, 9am–1pm Sun

This archaeological site is one of the largest Indigenous burial sites in the Caribbean. Of the 108 skeletons unearthed, many still lie in situ as they were found, and can be seen from a boardwalk. A museum displays artifacts. The neighboring Aldea Taína re-creates an Indigenous village with statues; locals re-enact Taíno life.

Museo Aborigen Chorro de Maíta

② Holguín

Home to colonial plazas, several churches, and museums, this industrious provincial capital is worth exploring (see pp28–9). Its most famous former resident was Calixto García, a general in the Wars of Independence (see p36). His house, now containing a museum, stands near Plaza Calixto García, where the Museo Provincial de Historia displays period pieces. Climb the steps to the top of Loma de la Cruz for splendid views. Mirador de Mayabe offers a grand mountain-top lunch.

③ Gibara

Once a wealthy port town, Gibara now draws much of its current income from a fishing fleet that harbors in picturesque Bahía de Bariay. The original city walls are now relics, but Parque Calixto García is home to a colonial church and museums of natural history and decorative arts. The town's white-painted houses lend the city its nickname, "Villa Blanca" (White Town) (see p29).

④ Santiago de Cuba

MAP P6 ■ Museo Ambiento Histórico: Calle Félix Pena 612; 2265 2652, 8am–5pm daily; adm

Graced by intriguing buildings, this now sprawling industrial city was Cuba's capital until 1553. Must-see sites include the Cathedral, Casa-Museo de Diego Velázquez, Museo Emilio Bacardí, and the Moncada barracks – a focus for Castro in 1953 (see p37). After the Haitian revolution in 1791, French and Haitian migrants fostered unique forms of architecture, music, and dance in the city, which is famed for its annual July carnivals.

Museo Emilio Bacardí, Santiago de Cuba

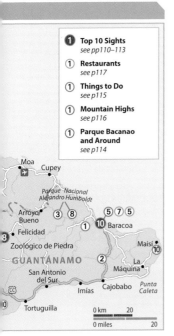

Moa
Cupey
Parque Nacional Alejandro Humboldt
Arroyo Bueno ③ ⑧ ⑤ ⑦ ⑤
Felicidad ① ⑩ Baracoa
Zoológico de Piedra
Maisí ⑩
GUANTÁNAMO ② La Máquina
San Antonio del Sur
Imías Cajobabo Punta Caleta
Tortuguilla

0 km 20
0 miles 20

Bayamo's colorful Plaza de la Revolución

5 Playa Guardalavaca

This beach zone, an hour's drive north of Holguín, was developed as a holiday resort in the 1980s and is now Cuba's third-largest resort destination. Development is focused on the beaches of Esmeralda (see p54), Yuraguanal, and Pesquero, and either side of flask-shaped Bahía de Naranjo. Trails provide insights into local ecology (see p29).

Sitio Histórico Birán

6 Sitio Histórico Birán

MAP N4 ▪ 2428 6902 ▪ Open 8am–3pm Tue–Sat (to noon Sun) ▪ Adm (guided tours available)

The Finca Manacas estate, outside Birán, where Fidel Castro was born and lived until his adolescence, belonged to his father Ángel Castro (see p40). The wooden mansion has been restored and is furnished with original family pieces. The grounds include Fidel's parents' graves, a former schoolhouse, and buildings, which were relocated to create an idealized village.

7 Bayamo

MAP N5 ▪ Parroquial Mayor de San Salvador: 2342 2514; open 8:30am–5pm Tue–Fri, 8:30am–noon Sat, 9am Sun (Mass) ▪ Casa Natal de Carlos Manuel de Céspedes: 2342 3864; open 9am–4pm Tue–Fri, 9am–noon Sat & Sun

Founded in 1513 by Diego Velázquez, Bayamo is Cuba's second-oldest city. In the early 19th century it was the cradle of revolt against Spanish rule. Much of the original city was destroyed in 1869, when citizens razed their town rather than surrender to the invading Spanish forces. Fortunately, many key sites survived this destruction, and today the restored historic core is a national monument. Most sights are concentrated around Parque Céspedes and Plaza del Himno, including the not-to-be-missed Parroquial Mayor de San Salvador church and the Casa Natal de Carlos Manuel de Céspedes.

COLUMBUS IN CUBA

Baracoans claim Christopher Columbus (right) landed at Puerto Santo and that the flat-topped mountain he described was El Yunque (see p33). Most experts, however, ascertain that the mountain was the Silla de Gibara and that Columbus landed in the Bahía de Bariay on October 28, 1492.

8 Zoológico de Piedra
MAP Q5 ■ Boquerón de Yateras ■ Open 8am–5pm daily ■ Adm

The name means "stone zoo," a term appropriate for the more than 400 life-size creatures displayed here. The animals, including lions, an elephant, a gorilla, and crocodiles, were carved from stone by coffee farmer Angel Iñigo, a self-taught sculptor who used photographs to hew the creatures. Iñigo also created entire vignettes such as monkeys picking fleas and Taínos killing a wild boar. The restaurant serves *criollo* meals.

The imposing facade of El Cobre

9 El Cobre
MAP P6 ■ 12 miles (19 km) northwest of Santiago ■ Sala de Milagros: 2234 6118; open 8am–6pm

This village is named after the copper (*cobre*) mined here in early colonial days. Pilgrims come to the Basílica de Nuestra Señora de la Caridad del Cobre (*see p31*), built in 1926, to ask favors of the Virgen de la Caridad, and leave ex votos (offerings) in the Sala de Milagros (Salon of Miracles).

10 Baracoa

Cuba's most easterly city, Baracoa (*see pp32–3*) is spectacularly set within a broad bay. The Hotel El Castillo (*see p129*), a former fortress, provides the best views in town. The city has a church with a cross that locals believe was brought over by Columbus. Baracoa is a good base for hiking and bird-watching, especially at Parque Nacional Alejandro Humboldt (*see p51*).

A DRIVE FROM SANTIAGO TO BARACOA

▶ MORNING

Leave early from **Santiago de Cuba** (*see p111*), taking the Autopista Nacional, which begins in the Vista Alegre district. Be careful on the freeway, which has plenty of potholes and traffic. After about 5 miles (8 km), exit at the signed junction for La Maya. The road passes through sugarcane fields, with the Sierra Baconao rising to the south. Continue east to Guantánamo, where sites of interest around Parque Martí can be explored in one hour. Stop for early lunch at La Ruina (*see p117*). Crossing the Río Bano, divert north to Boquerón de Yateras to reach the **Zoológico de Piedra**. Return to Guantánamo and turn east toward **Baracoa**. The road passes the entrance to **Mirador La Gobernadora** (*see p117*). Stop to look through the binoculars (for a price) over Guantánamo Bay.

AFTERNOON

Continue east via Playa Yateritas to Cajobabo. Here, turn south to reach Playita, where a museum recalls José Martí's return from exile. Visit the memorial at the spot where Martí landed with General Máximo Gómez (*see p37*). Beyond Cajobabo, the road snakes into the Sierra de Purial via **La Farola** (*see p116*). The mountain road is scenic but drive carefully, especially in fog and rain. At the summit, Alto de Coltillo, have a cup of hot coffee, and buy a bar of Baracoa chocolate or *cucurucho* from the roadside shacks before winding back down the mountain's north side toward a coastal plain.

See map on pp110–11

Parque Baconao and Around

 Playa Siboney
This pebbly beach frequented by locals has *casas particulares* that offer rooms overlooking the Caribbean *(see p55)*.

 Valle de la Prehistoria
MAP P6 ■ Carretera de Baconao, km 6.5 ■ Open 8am–5pm ■ Adm
Life-sized model dinosaurs cast in concrete and steel, plus a natural history museum, are found at this park *(see p56)*.

③ **Jardín Botánico**
MAP P6 ■ Viajes Cubanacán: Av. de las Américas & M, Santiago ■ 2264 2202 ■ Open 8am–4pm ■ Adm
Cubanacán offers tours to visit this elevated garden, with flowers that bloom all year round.

④ **Museo de Automóviles**
MAP P6 ■ Conjunto de Museos de la Punta, Carretera de Baconao, km 8.5 ■ Open 8am–5pm ■ Adm
Among the cars on display is the curious one-cylinder Maya Cuba. An adjoining museum displays around 2,500 toy cars.

⑤ **Prado de las Esculturas**
MAP P6 ■ Carretera a Siboney & Carretera de la Gran Piedra ■ Closed for renovation ■ Adm
A walking trail leads past metal artworks in this sculpture garden.

⑥ **Cafetal La Isabelica**
MAP P6 ■ Carretera de la Gran Piedra, km 14 ■ Open 8am–4pm ■ Adm
Learn about coffee production at this 18th-century coffee estate.

⑦ **Museo de la Guerra Hispano-Cubano-Norteamericano**
MAP P6 ■ Carretera Siboney, km 13 ■ 2239 9119 ■ Open 9am–5pm Mon–Sat ■ Adm
This museum has original weaponry and uniforms from the 1898 Spanish-American War *(see p47)*.

⑧ **Comunidad Artística Los Mamoncillos**
MAP Q6 ■ Playa Verraco, Carretera de Baconao
Shop for original works at this hamlet dedicated to arts and crafts.

⑨ **Pico Gran Piedra**
MAP Q6 ■ Carretera de la Gran Piedra, km 13
This huge boulder tops the 4,049-ft (1,234-m) mountain and offers great views as far as Haiti.

⑩ **Granita Siboney**
MAP P6 ■ Carretera Siboney, km 13 ■ 2239 9168 ■ Open 9am–5pm daily (to 1pm Mon) ■ Adm
Fidel Castro and his revolutionaries set out from this farmstead on July 26, 1953, to attack Moncada barracks *(see p37)*. A museum tells the tale.

Prado de las Esculturas

Things to Do

1 Dive at Marea del Portillo
MAP M6 ▪ Albacora Dive Center: Marea del Portillo ▪ 2359 7139

This modest beach resort will thrill scuba aficionados with its splendid dive sites. The highlight is the wreck of the Spanish warship, *Cristóbal Colón*, sunk in 1898.

2 Drive to Chivirico
MAP M6–P6

Soaring skyward from a teal-blue sea, the Sierra Maestra push up against a barren coast road linking Marea del Portillo with Santiago de Cuba. The stunning scenery is the perfect backdrop to the road.

3 Dance at the Casa de la Trova, Santiago

The epicenter of *son* music (see p58), Casa de la Trova has been a center of learning for top musicians. Paintings of famous artists adorn the walls.

4 Honor José Martí at Dos Ríos
MAP N5

The site of José Martí's martyrdom (see p37) is marked by an obelisk. The memorial, surrounded by white roses, is an allusion to Martí's famous poem, Cultivo una rosa blanca.

5 Hiking in Parque Nacional Desembarco del Granma

The site of the *Granma* landing (see p38), this park features trails through semi-arid forest with caves. Marine terraces offer great views (see p51).

6 Boat Ride at Yumurí
MAP R5

The Río Yumurí runs through coastal mountains and is a stunning setting for boat trips departing from the wharf at the river mouth. Negotiate a fee with the boat owners first.

Pristine beaches at Cayo Saetía island

7 Visit Cayo Saetía
MAP P4 ▪ 2451 6900

African game roam freely in the wilds of this small island with sensational white beaches. It was once a hunting preserve for the Communist elite.

8 Spot Birds at Parque Nacional Alejandro Humboldt
MAP R5 ▪ Ecotur: Calle Maceo 120, Baracoa ▪ 2164 2478 ▪ ecoturbc@enet.cu

Take a guided tour in search of the world's smallest bird, the bee hummingbird. Cool off in fresh water pools, and explore adjacent Taco Bay by boat.

9 Birding in Sierra Cristal

Sightings of colorful Cuban parrots and *tocororos* (see p52) are the rewards for bird enthusiasts on hikes through the montane forests of northeastern Cuba.

10 Watch the Sunrise at Punta Maisí
MAP R5

Accessed by a coastal road, the easternmost tip of Cuba is pinned by a lighthouse. The sun rises here 40 minutes before it does in Havana.

See map on pp110–11 ◄

Mountain Highs

Dramatic and striking flat-topped mountain of El Yunque, Baracoa

1 El Yunque
A unique flat top on El Yunque forms a dramatic backdrop to Baracoa, and you can hike to the summit. The views from the top are fabulous and worth the trip *(see p33)*.

2 La Farola
MAP R5
Experience a winding, breathtakingly steep drive up the mountain linking Guantánamo to Baracoa. Magnificent scenery awaits drivers, but extreme care is required on the switchbacks.

3 Parque Nacional Alejandro Humboldt
MAP R5 ▪ Ecotur: 2164 3665
Don sturdy footwear for the hike into the mountains of this park, which features *miradores* (lookouts) offering marvelous views. Guides are mandatory, and Ecotur can arrange them for you.

4 El Saltón
MAP N5 ▪ Villa El Saltón: 2256 9238
This ecotourism mountain resort offers trails, waterfalls, and superb bird-watching. The Villa El Saltón is a good base for exploring.

5 Pinares de Mayarí
MAP P5 ▪ 2445 5628
Accessed by a denuded road, this mountain resort *(see p51)* offers outdoor activities amid the pine forests, as well as around the Salto el Guayabo waterfall.

6 Parque Nacional Pico Turquino
MAP N6
Cuba's highest peak *(see p51)* is a challenging two-day ascent leading through various ecosystems, including a cloud forest.

7 Grupo Maniabón
MAP P4
Surrounded by *mogotes (see p17)*, this visually delightful mountain chain northeast of Holguín is best explored via a guided excursion.

8 La Comandancia de la Plata
Fidel Castro's former guerrilla head-quarters, hidden by thick forest and overhanging a ravine, are kept as they were five decades ago *(see p39)*.

9 Gran Piedra
MAP P6
The "Great Stone" *(see p114)* is a huge boulder balanced atop the ridge of the Sierra Baconao, and reached via a 454-step staircase. It offers panoramic views as far as Haiti.

10 Mayarí Arriba
MAP P6
The Museo Comandancia del Segundo Frente *(see p38)* recalls the years of the Revolution when the pine forests surrounding this town were the setting for guerrilla warfare in the Second Front, led by Raúl Castro. His grave has already been prepared in the mausoleum here.

Restaurants

1 El Palenquito
MAP P6 ▪ Av del Río 28 between Calle 6 y Carretera del Caney, Reparto Pastorita ▪ 2264 5220 ▪ $$$
This is the city's top barbecue spot for fresh meat and seafood platters in a garden setting.

2 Restaurante 1720
MAP N4 ▪ Calle Frexes 190, Holguín ▪ 2446 8150 ▪ $$
Located in a restored colonial mansion, Restaurante 1720 offers a creative menu that includes paella, and tasty creole shrimp in rum.

3 Restaurante El Morro
MAP P6 ▪ Parque Histórico El Morro, Santiago de Cuba ▪ 2269 1576 ▪ $$
This delightfully rustic restaurant sits atop a coastal headland. Eat your *criolla* lunch while enjoying the spectacular views from the terrace.

Restaurante El Morro

4 Restaurante Loma de la Cruz
MAP N4 ▪ Loma de la Cruz, Holguín ▪ 2447 1523 ▪ $$
Incomparable views over the city are offered at the Spanish *bodega*-style place. Try the tasty lamb enchilada.

5 Baracoando
MAP R5 ▪ Calle Flor Crombet 9, Baracoa ▪ $
Cuba's first and only vegan restaurant, Baracoando serves

PRICE CATEGORIES
For a three-course meal with half a bottle of wine (or equivalent meal), taxes, and extra charges.
$ under CUP$360 $$ CUP$360–600
$$$ over CUP$600

some of the country's freshest, tastiest food. There is no set menu and reservations are required.

6 St. Pauli
MAP P6 ▪ Calle Saco 605, Santiago de Cuba ▪ 2265 2292 ▪ $$
Hidden away a stone's throw west of Plaza Marte, this family restaurant serves excellent lobster, *ropa vieja*, and other Cuban staples.

7 La Cocina de Ortiz
MAP R5 ▪ Calle Rafael Trejo 15, Baracoa ▪ 5800 1237 ▪ $$
Chef Ineldis Trutié Ortiz trained at Havana's best restaurants before returning to his roots in Baracoa. Expect fresh seafood dishes and creative desserts.

8 Mesón La Cuchipapa
MAP N5 ▪ Parada entre Martí y Marmol, Bayamo ▪ 2341 1991 ▪ $$
A smart, rustic restaurant offering traditional Cuban *criolla* dishes and inventive cocktails with panache.

9 Restaurante Zunzún
MAP P6 ▪ Av. Manduley 159, Santiago de Cuba ▪ 2264 1528 ▪ $$
This atmospheric restaurant has a wide-ranging menu. Housed in a colonial mansion, enjoy your meal in the comfort of the air-conditioned salon or on the terrace outside.

10 La Ruina
MAP Q5 ▪ Calle Galixto García y Gulo, Guantánamo ▪ 2132 9565 ▪ $$
Housed in the shell of a colonial building, this popular *bodega*-style beer hall serves *comida criolla* (Puerto Rican cuisine).

See map on pp110–11 →

Streetsmart

Classic American car in Trinidad

Getting Around

Arriving by Air

Virgin Atlantic offers regular flights between London and Havana. Air France, Air Europa, Iberia, and KLM fly from Europe to Cuba, as do charter companies Air Berlin and Thomson. Air Canada, Cubana, and many charter companies connect Canada with the island, and US airlines offer scheduled services to Havana for licensed travelers. **Cubana Aviación** runs internal flights within the country. Fares are lower off-season, which runs from May to November, and for mid-week departures. As far as possible, it is best to book in advance.

Situated on the southern outskirts of Havana, **Aeropuerto Internacional José Martí** is Cuba's main airport. **Víazul** and **Shuttle Aeropuerto** buses take passengers into Havana. The second-most used airport is **Juan Gualberto Gómez** in Varadero.

There are other international airports around the country, but these are smaller and less-frequently used. They include **Aeropuerto Internacional Antonio Maceo** near Santiago de Cuba, Máximo Gómez in Ciego de Ávila, **Cayo Coco** in Cayo Coco, Ignacio Agramonte in Camagüey, and **Frank País** in Holguín.

Tourist taxis are present at international airports. As few taxi drivers use meters, it is customary to agree a fare before setting off. Decline offers from touts who may steer you toward private taxis.

Arriving by Sea

A few Caribbean-based cruise lines include Cuba in their itineraries, calling in at the port facilities of Havana and, infrequently, Santiago de Cuba and Cienfuegos.

Marinas around the island act as official ports of entry for independent sailors. Note that US sailors currently require prior approval from the Coast Guard and the **Office of Foreign Assets Control** (OFAC).

Domestic Air Travel

Cubana de Aviación has irregular connections between Havana, the provincial capitals, and key tourist centers around the island. Although these can be useful, demand often exceeds supply and services are unreliable.

Train Travel

Although Cuba has a large public railway network serving all the provincial capitals, trains are not the best way to get around. Service is unreliable and slow, with frequent delays and cancellations, timetables change without notice, and many carriages are old and uncomfortable. Tickets can only be purchased from **Viajeros** offices in towns and at stations up to 30 days in advance. Foreign visitors need to show passports.

Long-Distance Bus Travel

Buses are safe and reliable, and are the best way to get around Cuba. The **Ómnibus Nacionales** operates intercity Astro buses, but visitors are barred from using these. Instead, Víazul is the main bus company for visitors and connects most cities and resorts using modern air-conditioned coaches with restrooms. Fares are very reasonable, and children's fares are half-price. Reservations must be booked at least a few hours in advance, either online or at stations (card payment only). Services depart from the town's main bus station or plaza.

Public Transport

Public transport in Cuba is a mix of private and state-run services and there is no central public transport authority. Most cities operate buses, taxis, rudimentary *bicitaxis* (tricycles) and *camiones* (lorries). Of these, taxis and hop-on/hop-off sightseeing buses best serve visitors.

Buses

Most public buses (*guaguas* – pronounced gwah-wahs) are modern, but in provincial towns and cities the standard of buses varies wildly, ranging from luxurious air-conditioned cruisers to old and weary Soviet-era vehicles. Fares are incredibly cheap, but vehicles are usually crowded, and waiting times can be very long. Due to these many inconveniences, you'll find that very few visitors use public buses.

Bus travel is made easier in the capital, however, by the hop-on/hop-off air-conditioned tourist bus service, **HabanaBusTour**, with two different routes around town. Route 1 starts in Parque Central and travels west to Plaza de la Revolución, while Route 2 heads east to the Playas del Este. Other key towns and areas, including Viñales, Trinidad, Varadero, Santa María and Cayo Coco, also have hop-on/hop-off sightseeing buses.

Neighbouring towns and rural areas are served by camiones: crude conversions of prerevolutionary lorries. Privately owned, they are very cheap but usually extremely crowded and insufferably hot in summer months, with passengers often exposed to the elements.

Taxis

Cuba has multiple types of taxis. State-run yellow Taxis Cuba operate throughout the country, as do Cubataxi's yellow "tourist taxis". Prices are reasonable, especially outside Havana. Most drivers do not use their meters, preferring to negotiate a fare; you should agree the price before you start your trip. Taxis can be hailed outside major hotels and at taxi stands (piqueras) on the main squares, or radiodispatched by phone.

Private colectivo taxis, which are shared with other passengers and are licensed to operate like buses along fixed routes, pick up and drop off as many people as they can hold for a fixed fare. Vehicles tend to be beaten-up prerevolutionary classics or Soviet Ladas. Taxi Ruteros are black-and-yellow mini-buses that can be hailed along fixed routes.

The default mode of transport for short journeys within La Habana Vieja, Centro Habana, and provincial cities is the bicitaxi, a rickshaw like tricycle with shade-covered seats. They circulate around these areas, or can be found outside hotel entrances, and provide a fun, but slow, way to travel short distances. Be sure to negotiate the fare before departing as scamming of visitors is common.

Cocotaxis are open-air motorized tricycles found in key tourist destinations, such as Havana and Varadero. Roughly shaped like coconuts, they are aimed at tourists and do not have a good safety record. In Santiago de Cuba, private small motorcycles – moto-taxis – are the main form of taxi for single-person rides, but these are not always the safest option.

Classic pre-revolutionary American cars, easily recognizable by the Taxis Cuba or Gran Car sign and logo, are available for rent as chauffeured touring vehicles and taxis in cities. In Havana, these quirky cars can be hired on Parque Central and outside deluxe hotels. Ride-hailing apps such as La Nave and Bajanda are also becoming popular.

DIRECTORY

ARRIVING BY AIR

Aeropuerto Internacional Antonio Maceo
Santiago de Cuba
[22 69 8614

Aeropuerto Internacional José Martí
Havana
[7649 7151

Cayo Coco
[3330 9300

Cubana Aviación
w cubana.cu

Frank País
Holguín
[2445 8826

Juan Gualberto Gómez
Varadero
[45 24 7015

Shuttle Aeropuerto
[7649 7371

Víazul
[7266 4171
w viazul.wetransp.com

ARRIVING BY SEA

Office of Foreign Assets Control
w treas.gov/ofac

DOMESTIC AIR TRAVEL

Cubana de Aviación
Calle 23 No. 64, Havana
[7834 4446
w cubana.cu

TRAIN TRAVEL

Viajero
[7860 3165

BUSES

HabanaBusTour
[7838 3995

Boats and Ferries

Simple lanchas *(ferries)* link La Habana Vieja to the communities of Casablanca and Regla, charging a small fee in *pesos*. A similar service is offered to Cayo Granma, in Santiago de Cuba. High-speed hydrofoil catamarans offer a service to Isla de la Juventud from Surgidero de Batabanó, on the Caribbean shore south of Havana. Reservations must be made at least one day in advance at the **Viajero** office in Havana's Terminal de Ómnibus.

Driving

One of the best ways to see a lot of Cuba's hinterland is to travel by car, discovering places and scenery that it would be difficult to see on an organized tour or by public transport. Traffic is extremely light, and most Cubans are safe drivers. Make sure you are familiar with the rules of the road and have all the necessary documentation, as traffic police *(tránsitos)* are ubiquitous and efficient.

Cuba has an extensive network of paved roads. The one-lane main highway – the Carretera Central – runs through the centre of the island from Pinar del Río in the west to Guantánamo in the east. The country's main artery, it connects all the major cities. The disjointed Circuito Norte runs along the north shore and connects to the Carretera Central by feeder roads. A motorway *(autopista)* connects Havana to Pinar del Río and Santa Clara. Caution is required when driving as some roads are in bad condition and signage is often poor.

Car Rental

Car rental is widely available in Cuba. To rent a car in Cuba you must be over 21 and have a valid national driver's license or International Driver's Permit (IDP). Cuba's car rental agencies are all state-run and no international companies are represented. Any responsibility pertaining to the car maintenance is placed on the renters by contract. It's wise to make reservations well in advance as vehicles are in short supply, especially in high season. Cars can also be picked up and dropped off at most of the airports.

Prices are expensive, although discounts apply for rentals of a week or longer. A deposit is required, and you must pay in advance in cash for the first tank of fuel. The three rental agencies (Cubacar, **Havanautos** and **Rex**) operated by **Transtur** don't mind if you return the vehicle with an empty tank; **Via** requires that the vehicle be returned with the same amount of fuel as when you depart. You may be required to take the car to a local office at a specific designated kilometre reading (noted on your contract as *aviso próximo mantanimiento*). A $50 fine usually applies for failure to honour this. For exploring certain parts of the island, including the extreme west and far east, it may be best to hire a four-wheel drive (off-roader) to negotiate the pitted roads.

International insurance coverage is invalid in Cuba. You will be required to purchase either limited Collision Damage Waiver (CDW) or fully comprehensive insurance, but note that the "comprehensive" option has limitations, and your insurance may be invalidated if you are found guilty of causing an accident or if your blood alcohol concentration level is found to exceed 0.05 per cent.

Rules of the Road

Drive on the right, use the left lane only for passing and yield to traffic from the right. Seat belts are required for all front-seat passengers. A strict drink-drive policy is enforced, and it is wise to avoid all alcohol if intending to drive.

During the day, the use of headlights is not officially permitted except during heavy rain. Only emergency vehicles are allowed to use headlights in the daytime.

Tránsito (traffic police) enforce speed limits of 30 mph (48 km/h) in towns, 37 mph (59 km/h) on rural roads, 55 mph (88 km/h) on highways, and 62 mph (98 km/h) on freeways. Every so often on the *autopista* (motorway) you will see signs telling you to reduce your speed to around 50 km/h (30 mph). Do not ignore these instructions, as they are often followed by road blocks. In general, the police are quite tolerant of tourists, but being caught speeding may invalidate your car insurance so always stick to the limit.

In the event of an accident or breakdown, switch on your hazard warning lights and place a warning triangle or small branches, Cuban-style, 50 m (164 ft) behind your vehicle. If you are involved in an accident, do not move your vehicle. Accidents involving injury or death are treated as crimes – you may not be allowed to leave Cuba until a trial is held, often resulting in a prison term for the guilty party. Contact your embassy immediately if you are involved in a fatal accident on the road.

At any time of day, take extra care after rainy weather, because road surfaces may become flooded. In mountain areas there may be some danger of falling rocks. When driving in Havana, stay alert and watch out for the cyclists and pedestrians. Keep speeds low and look out for potholes and bumps.

An excellent and detailed road atlas, *Guía de Carreteras*, is sold throughout Cuba at Infotur offices. Ask your car hire company for a free *automapa*, which shows where the Servi-Cupet service stations are located across the island.

Parking

Theft of car parts (but rarely of cars) is a potential problem in Cuba, especially at night. Always park your car in a *parqueo* (designated car park) wherever possible as almost all of these will have a *custodio* (guard), or park on the roadside if it is attended by a state-employed *custodio* (easily identified by their red waistcoats). Private *custodios* can also be hired to watch your car overnight for a fee.

Hitchhiking

Hitchhiking *(pedir botella)* in town and in the countryside is common among Cubans of all ages. Although this is a normal way of life in Cuba, it is not recommended for tourists. If you do decide to hitchhike, always consider your own safety before entering an unknown vehicle.

Bicycle and Motorcycle Hire

Although cycling is well established in provincial cities, few Habaneros ride bicycles. Nonetheless, several companies in Havana, such as Bike Rentals & Tours, rent bicycles to visitors.

Many travelers bring their own bicycles to the island. If you do this, a sturdy lock is essential and be sure to park in bicycle garages *(bici parqueos)* wherever available to avoid potential thefts. Bicycle mechanics can easily be found anywhere in the country, but it's wise to bring all the spare parts you may need.

No motorcycles are available for rent in Cuba, but scooters can be hired in most cities and tourist resorts from state tour agencies. No license is required.

Walking

Few Cubans own cars and many people get around on foot. Walking is the best way of soaking up the sights, sounds and local life in towns and cities. Cuba's compact city centers in particular are perfect for exploring on foot. Though Havana is an immense city, if you are staying in the city centre, it's feasible to do most of your exploring on foot. If you begin to tire, it's easy enough to flag down a taxi.

Licensed guides can be hired in Old Havana, Trinidad, and Santiago de Cuba. You may be approached by people purporting to be guides, so always make sure they are licensed.

Outside of the cities, there are a number of national parks with stunning landscapes and wildlife. Trails tend to be poorly maintained so joining a guided hike led by a local is the best option.

DIRECTORY

BOATS AND FERRIES

Viajero
📞 7870 0939

CAR RENTAL

Havanautos
🌐 havanautos.com

Rex
🌐 rexcarrental.com

Transtur
🌐 rentcarcuba.com

Via
🌐 carrentalcuba.com

Practical Information

Passports and Visas

For entry requirements, including visas, consult your nearest Cuban embassy. EU nationals and citizens of the UK, US, Canada, Australia and New Zealand need a Tourist Card for stays of up to 30 days. These are issued by airlines, travel agencies and Cuban consulates and are extendable for an additional 30 days when you are on the island. All visitors must have medical insurance and fill out an online form to register their immigration and health status on the **D'Viajeros** website before arrival.

In addition to a Tourist Card, US citizens (and all those departing US soil for Cuba) need a "general licence" issued by the **Office of Foreign Assets Control**, to visit Cuba.

Government Advice

Now more than ever, it is important to consult your government's advice before traveling. The **UK Foreign and Common-wealth Office**, the **US State Department**, and the **Australian Department of Foreign Affairs and Trade** offer the latest information on security, health and local regulations.

Customs Information

You can find information on the laws relating to goods and currency taken in or out Cuba on the **Cuba Travel** tourist information website. Visitors are allowed to bring in 200 cigarettes and 6 pints (3 liters) of spirits duty free, as well as 44 lb (20 kg) of personal belongings into the country. Pack personal medicines in their original packaging. Customs searches in Cuba can be rigorous.

Insurance

All visitors must have pre-arranged medical insurance as a condition of entry to Cuba. As well as medical insurance, we recommend taking out a comprehensive policy covering theft, loss of belongings, cancellations and delays.

Health

Proof of medical insurance is required for entry to Cuba. Cuba's healthcare system is quite good but pharmaceuticals are often in short supply. Be sure to bring any medicine you know you will need during your stay, as well as any prescriptions you have for these, and plenty of sunscreen and insect repellent. It is also wise to bring a small medical kit with you. If you need additional medicinal supplies or advice about minor ailments, seek out an International Pharmacy (*Farmacia Internacional*), found in major cities and resorts.

Emergency medical care for visitors is given at International Clinics (*Clínicas Internacionales*), and at local hospitals. You will need to show your medical insurance documents. You may be charged a nominal fee for any treatment that you receive. Keep receipts to reclaim the cost from your insurance company later. Most tourist hotels will also have a doctor or nurse on call.

Do not drink the tap water in Cuba. Some people prefer not to brush their teeth with it. You should also make sure that ice cubes are made from purified water. Bottled water can be bought and is widely available. Do not drink from a bottle of water that is unsealed, as it may have been refilled with tap water.

No inoculations are needed for Cuba, but it is recommended that you are inoculated against tetanus, typhoid and hepatitis A and B. For information regarding COVID-19 vaccination requirements, consult government advice.

Smoking, Alcohol and Drugs

Smoking is officially banned in many enclosed public spaces, including restaurants, but this is rarely enforced. The possession of illegal drugs is prohibited and could result in a prison sentence as Cuba has zero tolerance.

Cuba has a strict limit of 0.05 per cent BAC (blood alcohol content) for drivers. This means that you cannot drink more than a small beer or tot of rum if you plan to drive. Drivers who cause an accident and have a BAC in excess of this limit are likely to be given a prison sentence.

ID

By law you must carry identification with you at all times in Cuba. A photocopy of your passport photo page and tourist card should suffice. If you are stopped by the police you may need to present your original passport within 24 hours.

Personal Security

Cuba is a safe place to visit and, unlike in many other parts of Latin America, violent crime is rare. However, petty crime does take place. Pickpockets are known to work crowded city centres, tourist spots and public transport. Use your common sense, keep your belongings close and be alert to your surrounds. If you have anything stolen, report the crime within 24 hours to the nearest police station and take your passport with you. If you need to make an insurance claim, get a copy of the crime report (denuncia). Contact your embassy if your passport is stolen, or in the event of a serious crime or accident.

Homosexuality was legalized in Cuba in 1979 but there is generally a conservative stance to LGBTQ+ people in smaller towns and rural areas where overt displays of affection may attract unwanted attention. Since the 1990s, attitudes have changed considerably in Havana and other large cities, however. The main LGBTQ+ scenes are in Havana's Vedado neighbourhood and along the Malacón, on Mi Cayito Beach and in the town of Santa Clara.

Machismo is ingrained in Cuba's male culture. This is generally limited to flirtatious behavior toward women but can also include expressions of bravado and even aggression intended to demonstrate male pride. If you feel threatened, head straight for the nearest police station.

Ambulance, **police** and **fire** services can be contacted for emergencies. **Asistur** exists to help tourists in distress and has offices in most tourist centers. The **Consultoría Jurídica Internacional** can provide legal help and has branches in all of Cuba's main cities.

In the event of a serious car accident, call the traffic police (tránsito) and your car-rental company. It is also wise to contact your embassy.

Travelers with Specific Requirements

Cuba can be tricky to navigate for those with physical, hearing or visual impairment. While most modern and renovated hotels provide amenities for wheelchair-users, many historic buildings do not have wheelchair access or lifts. The centre of Havana has occasional kerb ramps but these are even rarer in provincial towns. There are no adapted buses or taxis. On the plus side, Cubans are very accommodating, and do their best to make things as easy as possible for everyone.

DIRECTORY

PASSPORTS AND VISAS

D'Viajeros
w dviajeros.mitrans.gob.cu

Office of Foreign Assets Control
w treasury.gov/resource-center/sanctions/Programs/pages/cuba.aspxe

GOVERNMENT ADVICE

Australian Department of Foreign Affairs and Trade
w smartraveller.gov.au

UK Foreign and Commonwealth Office
w gov.uk/foreign-travel-advice

US State Department
w travel.state.gov/

CUSTOMS INFORMATION

Cuba Travel
w cubatravel.cu

PERSONAL SECURITY

Ambulance
(104

Asistur
(7866 4499

Consultoría Jurídica Internacional
(7204 8402

Fire
(105

Police
(106

Time Zone

Cuba is on Eastern Standard Time (EST) and is 5 hours behind Greenwich Mean Time (GMT), the same as New York and Miami. Daylight saving time operates from May to October.

Money

The official currency is the Cuban peso (CUP), shown as $ in this guide. There is also a digital, government-approved currency called Moneda Libremente Convertibile (MLC) that can be used in MLC-designated shops, but it is rarely adopted by tourists. Since Cuba abolished convertible pesos and took US dollars out of circulation in 2021, there has been huge inflation and the value of the local currency fluctuates widely. Check the exchange rate before your trip and prepare for prices (including those in this book) to be more or less expensive than expected. You may find that privately owned businesses accept payment at a more favourable exchange rate than the official one.

Major credit cards (except cards issued or processed by US banks) are accepted in hotels, state-run restaurants, and tourist-oriented shops. An 11 per cent service charge may apply. It is best to bring your spending money in cash and in euros, the preferred foreign currency (Canadian dollars and pounds stirling are accepted by some private businesses). Convert some euros into CUP for small purchases, to tip, and for payments at state-run establishments. It is customary to tip 10 per cent of the bill in restaurants. It is not usual to tip taxi drivers.

Electrical Appliances

Cuba's erratic electricity supply works on a 110-volt system, as in the US and Canada, although some outlets are 220-volt and are usually marked. Plugs are the two-pin North American type, so European visitors will need to bring adaptors.

Mobile Phones and Wi-Fi

Wi-Fi is widely available in most hotels, parks and squares, as well as some cafés and restaurants, across Cuba. All users must purchase a Nauta access card issued by **ETECSA**, the state telecommunications company. These cards can be purchased at ETESCA stores and at major hotels, and include a username and password for a specific number of hours' use. A growing number of hotels offer free Wi-Fi.

Visitors bringing mobile phones to Cuba should check with their service providers to determine if they will work in Cuba and if they will be subject to roaming charges. A tourist SIM card, which can be purchased from **Cubacel** stores for mobile data, local calls and messages within Cuba, is good value and highly recommended.

Postal Services

Mail is extremely slow. Every town has a post office, and most tourist hotels also sell stamps (estampillas) or prepaid postcards. If sending anything of value or importance, use DHL, which has offices in all major cities.

Weather

Cuba's tourist season runs from December to April, when airfares, accommodations, and car rentals are at their most expensive. This period is less hot than the rest of the year, but temperatures in January can reach 79°F (26°C). The hurricane season in Cuba lasts from June to November.

It is worth packing a sweater or lightweight jacket for heavily air-conditioned restaurants, chilly winter nights, and visits to mountainous regions. Long-sleeved clothing and mosquito repellent help guard against mosquitoes. Sunscreen, a hat, and sunglasses are also essential.

Opening Hours

Most offices are open 8:30am–12:30pm and 1:30–5:30pm Monday to Friday. Shops usually remain open 8:30am–5:30pm Monday to Saturday. Banks typically open 8:30am–noon and 1:30–3pm Monday to Friday, and then 8:30–10:30am on Saturdays. Museums hours vary widely, but bear in mind that many are closed on Mondays. Many shops

COVID-19 Increased rates of infection may result in temporary opening hours and/or closures. Always check ahead before visiting museums, attractions and hospitality venues.

close on January 1 and 2, July 26, October 10, and December 25.

Visitor Information

Cuba Travel *(see p125)* provides information on the country. For details on events held in Cuba, visit **OnCuba**, a monthly online magazine with an events calendar, and **La Papeleta**, which covers cultural events.

Many Cuban websites are run by the state, and care should be taken if booking online. US websites are now permitted to accept bookings for trips to Cuba, but anyone traveling from the US should check the US State Department website *(see p125)* for a list of restricted entities and services, including the likes of boat trips, museums and tours.

Organized tours are a great way of experiencing the multiple sides of Cuba. Choose a reputable agency, such as **Journey Latin America** or **Cubania** if you prefer your travel arrangements to be pre-arranged. **Cuba Private Travel** and **Cuba Candela** tailor trips for specific interests, such as cooking, art and music. Cuba Candela also organizes social impact tours that offer an insight into local communities and activities such as beach clean-ups.

For more information on eco-tourism in Cuba, visit the **Ecotur** website.

Local Customs

Cuba is a tolerant country but social attitudes are rather conservative. Nudism and topless bathing are not allowed on most beaches.

The Cuban government is highly sensitive to criticism. For this reason, Cubans may be wary of discussing politics with people they do not know or trust. Although things have eased up considerably in recent years, be understanding if people are reluctant to discuss politics openly.

Most churches and cathedrals permit visitors during Sunday Mass and entrance to churches is free. Although Cuba is officially a secular state, it retains a strong Catholic identity, and Afro-Cuban religions such as Santería are even more firmly entrenched. When visiting religious buildings ensure that you are dressed modestly, with your knees and shoulders covered.

Language

Spanish is the official language in Cuba, but much of the population in cities speaks English, as well as many other languages. Locals appreciate visitors' efforts to speak Spanish, even if only a few words.

Taxes and Refunds

No taxes apply on purchases, nor is there a departure tax. However, many paintings incur a $3 fee by customs at the airport upon departure.

Booking Accommodation

In the summer months the state-run hotels fill up fast, and prices are inflated. Local *casas particulares* (private B&Bs) offer better bargains compared to hotels, and there is a huge selection for every budget. Many *casas* maintain websites, or are represented by agencies such as **Airbnb** and **CubaCasa**.

DIRECTORY

MOBILE PHONES AND WI-FI

Cubacel
w etecsa.cu/telefonia_movil

ETECSA
w etecsa.cu/es/visitantes/cubaceltur

VISITOR INFORMATION

Cuba Candela
w cubacandela.com

Cuba Private Travel
w cubaprivatetravel.com

Cubania
w cubaniatravel.com

Ecotur
w ecotur.cuba.tur.cu

Journey Latin America
w journeylatinamerica.co.uk

OnCuba
w oncubanews.com

La Papeleta
w lapapeleta.cu

BOOKING ACCOMMODATION

AirBnB
w airbnb.com

CubaCasa
w cubacasa.co.uk

Places to Stay

PRICE CATEGORIES
For a standard double room per night (with breakfast if included), taxes, and extra charges.

$ under CUP$1,250 $$ CUP$1,250–3,750 $$$ over CUP$3,750

Havana Hotels

Hostal Los Frailes
MAP X2 ■ Calle Brasil between Oficios & Mercaderes, La Habana Vieja ■ 7862 9383 ■ www.gaviotahotels.com ■ $
Themed as a monastery with staff that dress as monks, this hotel has cozy rooms with wrought-iron furnishings surrounding a patio. There is no restaurant, but nearby Plaza Vieja has several options.

Hotel Raquel
MAP X2 ■ Amargura & San Ignacio, La Habana Vieja ■ 7860 8280 ■ www.gaviotahotels.com ■ $$
A stylish historic hotel with Art Nouveau decor and an excellent location just one block from Plaza Vieja. Facilities include a solarium and a gym.

Gran Hotel Kempinski-Manzana
MAP V5 ■ Calle San Rafael between Monserrate & Zulueta, La Habana Vieja ■ 7869 9100 ■ $$$
Opened in 2017 as Cuba's most deluxe hotel, this hotel offers luxurious accommodations, a chic shopping gallery, a rooftop pool, a restaurant, and bar.

Hotel Capri
MAP U1 ■ Calle 21 esq. N, Vedado ■ 7839 7200 ■ www.nh-hotels.com ■ $$$
Reopened in 2014 after a five-year renovation, this former Mobster-run Modernist hotel now gleams afresh. Located in the heart of the city, this is the ideal base to explore the city's nightlife.

Hotel Florida
MAP X1 ■ Calle Obispo 252, La Habana Vieja ■ 7862 4117 ■ www.gaviotahotels.com ■ $$$
A magnificent building and a haven of peace on La Habana Vieja's busiest street, this sumptuous hotel is centered on a courtyard. It has spacious rooms furnished in colonial style with wrought-iron beds.

Hotel Iberostar Parque Central
MAP W1 ■ Calle Neptuno between Prado & Zulueta ■ 7860 6631 ■ www.iberostar.com ■ $$$
This luxury option overlooks Havana's liveliest square with elegant rooms that feature reproduction antiques. It has a classy lobby bar, two fine restaurants, boutiques, and two rooftop swimming pools. Popular with tour groups.

Hotel Nacional
MAP U1 ■ Calle O & 21, Vedado ■ 7836 3564 ■ www.hotelnacionaldecuba.com ■ $$$
Built in the 1930s, this grande dame is promoted as Havana's top hotel. It offers four restaurants and six bars, including a lovely garden terrace bar and the Cabaret Parisien, as well as two large swimming pools. Many rooms are dowdy, so take an executive floor room.

SO/ Paseo del Prado La Habana
MAP W1 ■ Corner of Prado and Malecón, La Habana Vieja ■ 7823 2400 ■ www.all.accor.com ■ $$$
A five-star hotel offering panoramic views of the Atlantic and Malecón. The rooms embrace contemporary decor and are inspired by Cuba's ballet and salsa music. A rooftop infinity pool, bar, and in-house chocolatería complete the picture.

Hotel Tryp Habana Libre
MAP U1 ■ Calle L & Av. 23, Vedado ■ 7834 6100 ■ www.meliacuba.com ■ $$
The key attractions of this 1950s high-rise in the heart of Vedado include a bank, a leading nightclub, a business center, tour desks, and a pool. The refurbished rooms are comfortable and contemporary in style.

Meliá Cohiba
MAP S1 ■ Paseo at Av. 1ra, Vedado ■ 7833-3636 ■ www.meliacuba.com ■ $$$
The business hotel par excellence in Havana, this modern Spanish-run place has top facilities, with deluxe rooms, excellent restaurants, and a vast swimming pool.

Town Center Hotels

Hotel Camino de Hierro, Camagüey
MAP L3 ▪ Plaza de la Solidaridad ▪ 3228 4264 ▪ www.hoteles cubanacan.com ▪ $$
A delightful newcomer in the heart of the historic district, this restored and rambling hotel has a graceful lobby and gourmet restaurant, and offers pleasantly furnished rooms with modern bathrooms.

Hotel Casa Granda, Santiago de Cuba
MAP P6 ▪ Calle Heredia 201 ▪ 2268 6600 ▪ www.iberostar.com ▪ $$
This handsome hotel on the main square offers refurbished rooms with reproduction antique furniture and modern accoutrements. The restaurant serves gourmet cuisine, and the terrace bar offers great views and a lively social scene.

Gran Hotel, Camagüey
MAP L3 ▪ Calle Maceo 67 ▪ 3229 2093 ▪ www.meliacuba.com ▪ $$
This is a classic hotel that has been restored to its former grandeur. The top-floor restaurant has good views and serves excellent buffets. The furnished, air-conditioned rooms offer safes, satellite TVs, and modern bathrooms.

Hotel El Castillo, Baracoa
MAP R5 ▪ Loma de Paraíso ▪ 2164 5165 ▪ www.gaviotahotels.com ▪ $$
The place to stay for postcard views of Baracoa and the unique El Yunque mountain (see p33), the rooms in this former fortress are comfortable and well-appointed with colonial furnishings. The restaurant is one of the best state-run options in town. A pool and tour desk are bonuses. It's only a two-minute walk into town, this involves a hike up and down a steep driveway or staircase.

Hotel E Martí, Guantánamo
MAP Q5 ▪ Calle Calixto García at Aguilera ▪ 2132 9500 ▪ $$
This simple hotel is situated next to Plaza Martí in the heart of town. It has modestly furnished rooms with modern bathrooms, and a pleasant restaurant.

Hotel Rijo, Sancti Spíritus
MAP J3 ▪ Calle Honorato del Castillo 12 ▪ 4132 8588 ▪ www.islazul hotels.com ▪ $$
A delightful 19th-century conversion on a charming plaza, this bargain-priced option has spacious, comfortable rooms with modern marble bathrooms. A satisfying and hearty breakfast is provided. There is an excellent restaurant on site too.

Hotel E Royalton, Bayamo
MAP N5 ▪ Calle Maceo 53 ▪ 2342 2290 ▪ www.islazul.cu ▪ $$
Built in the 1940s, this hotel is centrally located on the main square. The air-conditioned rooms, though not fancy, are comfortable, with TVs and en suite bathrooms.

Hotel E Vueltabajo, Pinar del Río
MAP B3 ▪ Calle Martí 103 ▪ 4875 9381 ▪ www.islazul.cu ▪ $$
This small hotel with spacious, simple rooms has a no-frills restaurant and bar. Rooms with a balcony cost a little more. Its downtown location is handy, but street noise can be a nuisance.

Hotel Jagua, Cienfuegos
MAP G3 ▪ Calle 37 between 0 & 2 ▪ 4355 1003 ▪ www.melia cuba.com ▪ $$
Managed since 2017 by Spain's Meliá chain, this 1950s Modernist high-rise has balconies with superb views to each side, as well as a sensational pool.

Hotel E San Basilio, Santiago de Cuba
MAP P6 ▪ Calle San Basilio 403 ▪ 2265 1702 ▪ www.hoteles cubanacan.com ▪ $$
A cozy hotel close to Parque Céspedes, this colonial mansion has a restaurant and 24-hour bar, plus a patio overlooking the square. The clean rooms are simple, with phones, safes, and TVs.

Iberostar Heritage Grand Trinidad, Trinidad
MAP H4 ▪ Calle Martí 262 ▪ 4199 6070 ▪ www.iberostar.com ▪ $$$
This deluxe, inner-city hotel has a gleaming marble staircase leading to 45 luxurious rooms and a restaurant that is one of the finest outside Havana. Added draws include a billiards room and cigar lounge.

Rural Hotels

Hotel Hanabanilla, Sierra Escambra

MAP H3 ■ Embalse Hanabanilla ■ 4220 8461 ■ www.islazulhotels.com ■ $$

A stunning lakeside setting in the foothills of the Sierra Escambray make up for the dull architecture of this Soviet-inspired two-star hotel. Rooms are refurbished, with modern amenities. Local tours are offered. It can get noisy on weekends.

Hotel Finca La Belén, El Pilar

MAP L4 ■ Comunidad El Pilar ■ 3286 4349 ■ reservas1@cmg.ecotur.tur.cu ■ $

This off-the-beaten-track hotel in Sierra del Chorillo, southeast of Camagüey city, appeals to nature lovers. The five spacious rooms have modern bathrooms, and there is a cozy lounge as well as a pool.

Villa Pinares de Mayarí, Pinares de Mayarí

MAP P5 ■ Loma La Mensura ■ 2445 5628 ■ www.gaviotahotels.com ■ $

A charming mountain resort offering hiking, mountain biking, and bird-watching. Set amid pine forests near lakes and waterfalls, it can only be reached via a daunting unpaved road.

Faro de Maisí, Punta Maisí

MAP R5 ■ Punta Maisí, Guantánamo ■ 2168 9605 ■ www.islazul.cu ■ $

Opened in 2017, this lovely little hotel is located near the very eastern tip of Cuba. It has 20 rooms and is a great base for nature activities.

Horizontes Villa Soroa, Soroa

MAP C2 ■ Carretera de Soroa, km 8 ■ 4852 3534 ■ www.hotelescubanacan.com ■ $$

Surrounded by forested hills, this bucolic option offers a lovely setting, with leafy grounds that slope down to a swimming pool.

Hotel La Moka, Las Terrazas

MAP C2 ■ Autopista Habana-Pinar del Río, km 51 ■ 4857 8602 ■ www.lasterrazas.cu ■ $$

Poised over Las Terrazas village and shrouded in woodland, this colonial-themed hotel focuses on ecotourism, with a lobby that is built around a tree. The spacious rooms offer scenic forest views.

Hotel Las Jazmines, Viñales

MAP B2 ■ Carretera a Viñales, km 23 ■ 4879 6133 ■ www.hotelescubanacan.com ■ $$

Housed in an original 1950s Neo-Colonial pink structure, this hotel has a spectacular hilltop setting that guarantees incredible views. Of the three room types available, the most comfortable are those in the modern annex.

Rancho Charco Azul, Artemisa

MAP D2 ■ Cayajabos, 9 miles (14km) W of Artemisa ■ 7206 2981 ■ $$

A peaceful country retreat, this converted coralstone mansion is at the center of a horse-breeding facility. It opened in 2016 as an eco-friendly hotel offering four rooms and eight chalets. Modern facilities include a swimming pool and dining. Guests are welcome to enjoy horseback riding.

Rancho San Vicente, Viñales

MAP B2 ■ Carretera a Puerto Esperanza, km 33 ■ 4879 6201 ■ www.hotelescubanacan.com ■ $$

This uncomplicated refuge in a wooded valley features simple air-conditioned cabins, with porches and huge windows. A lovely restaurant overlooks the swimming pool. There are several modern rooms in the building set opposite this hotel.

Villa Cayo Saetía, Cayo Saetía

MAP P4 ■ Cayo Saetía ■ 2451 6900 ■ www.gaviotahotels.com ■ $$

This beachside cabin complex is on a forested island once used for hunting by Communist officials, hence the abundance of African wildlife. The rustic restaurant is adorned with animal heads.

Villa El Saltón, El Saltón

MAP N5 ■ Carretera Filé, Tercer Frente ■ 2256 9238 ■ www.campismo popular.cu ■ $

Focused on ecotourism, this riverside hotel, surrounded by forest, offers guided hikes and bird-watching trips. The rooms are simply furnished but have satellite TV. The restaurant overlooks a waterfall.

Villa San José del Lago, Yaguajay

MAP J2 ■ Av. Antonio Guiteras ■ 4154 6108 ■ www.islazulhotels.com ■ $

On the north coast road of Sancti Spíritus province, this peaceful complex features thermal swimming pools and a lake with rowboats and flamingos. Air-conditioned cabins are simple yet comfy. The place comes alive on weekends.

Beach Hotels

Iberostar Daiquirí, Cayo Guillermo

MAP K2 ■ Ciego de Ávila, Cayo Guillermo ■ 3331 0650 ■ www.iberostar. com ■ $$$

Refurbished since 2017's Hurricane Irma, this handsome 312-room all-inclusive resort is set in lush grounds and has a full range of watersports, plus excellent children's facilities. It offers cabaret and other themed shows in the evenings.

Villa Maguana, Playa Maguana

MAP R5 ■ Baracoa–Moa road, km 20 ■ 2162 7204 ■ www.gaviota hotels. com ■ $$

This hotel was entirely rebuilt after Hurricane Irma. Four rustic, two-story villas sit in dense foliage near a private cove with a white-sand beach. Rooms are simple and comfortably furnished.

Brisas Trinidad del Mar, Playa Ancón

MAP H4 ■ Península Ancón ■ 4199 6504 ■ www.memoriesresorts. com ■ $$
The architecture at this modern, all-inclusive hotel integrates Neo-Classical elements inspired by the colonial buildings of nearby Trinidad. Rooms have modern amenities.

Hotel Cayo Levisa, Pinar del Río

MAP B3 ■ Palma Rubia, La Palma ■ 4875 6501 ■ www.hotelescubana can.com ■ $$

This hotel, on the pristine island of Cayo Levisa, is accessed by boat from the mainland. It offers three types of beachfront accommodation, including fourplex wooden villas. Guests can enjoy activities such as diving and snorkeling in calm turquoise waters. The restaurant caters to day visitors as well as guests.

Memories Varadero, Varadero

MAP F2 ■ Punta Hicacos, Autopista del Sur Final ■ 4566 7599 ■ www.memo riesresorts.com ■ $$$

This deluxe all-inclusive resort has bright decor. Rooms feature state-of-the-art amenities, and the pool has a huge spiral waterslide. However, its location at the remote eastern tip of the peninsula is a long way from town.

Iberostar Selection, Ensenachos

MAP J1 ■ Cayo Ensenachos, Cayos Villa Clara ■ 4235 0300 ■ www.iberostar.com ■ $$$

This is one of Cuba's most luxurious all-inclusive resorts, spread out over miles of grounds; as a result, many rooms are a considerable walk from the beach. A highlight is the children's water park.

Mansión Xanadu, Varadero

MAP F2 ■ Autopista del Sur, km 8.5 ■ 4566 8482 ■ www.varaderogolfclub. com ■ $$$

In the former mansion of the DuPont family, this all-inclusive hotel has six huge rooms with private balconies, a fine restaurant, and a bar with live music. Guests get golf privileges at the club.

Meliá Cayo Coco, Cayo Coco

MAP K2 ■ Cayo Coco ■ 3330 1180 ■ www. meliacuba.com ■ $$$

A chic all-inclusive that outshines most of the other hotels on the island. Refurbished in 2017, it caters to adults only, and room options include two-story cabins above a natural seawater lagoon. Guests have a choice of four restaurants.

Meliá Cayo Santa María, Cayo Santa María

MAP J1 ■ 4235 0500 ■ www.meliacuba.com ■ $$$

Elegant and all-inclusive, with a vast pool complex, this hotel offers a choice of gourmet restaurants, lively entertainment, and plenty of watersports.

Meliá Marina Varadero, Varadero

MAP F2 ■ Autopista del Sur y Final ■ 4566 7330 ■ www.meliacuba.com ■ $$$

Near the far eastern end of the peninsula, this sensational luxury hotel overlooks Cuba's largest marina. It has beautiful rooms, multiple gourmet restaurants, and tranquil spa facilities.

For a key to hotel price categories see p128

Paradisus Río de Oro, Guardalavaca

MAP P4 ▪ Playa Esmeralda ▪ 2443 0090 ▪ www.meliacuba.com ▪ $$$

This smart and luxurious adults-only beach hotel is built around a large swimming pool. Facilities include a spa and secret beach coves.

Hotel Cayo Largo del Sol, Cayo Largo

MAP F4 ▪ Playa Lindamar ▪ 4524 8260 ▪ $$$

A lovely all-inclusive resort on a spectacular stretch of white sand. Sol Cayo Largo has a pool and several restaurants. The rooms are painted in bright pastel colors.

Budget Hotels

Camagüey Colón, Camagüey

MAP L3 ▪ Av. República 472 ▪ 3225 1520 ▪ www. meliacuba.com ▪ $$

Opened in 1926, the restored Hotel Colón has a gleaming mahogany bar, which is a great place for cocktails, while the restaurant is considered one of the city's most elegant. One room is equipped for travelers with specific needs.

Hotel Rex, Santiago de Cuba

MAP P6 ▪ Av. Garzón 10 ▪ 2268 7092 ▪ www. islazulhotels.com ▪ $

This historic hotel, which has been refurbished in a modern fashion, offers great value for money. It has a stylish restaurant and bar and is the only hotel in Santiago de Cuba offering Wi-Fi across its entire premises.

Hotel E Central Viñales

MAP B2 ▪ Calle Salvador Cisneros, corner of Ceferino Fernández ▪ 4869 5815 ▪ $$

In the heart of the small town of Viñales, Hotel E Central, with 23 rooms, offers a front-row seat to local activity.

Hotel E La Ronda, Trinidad

MAP H4 ▪ Calle Martí 242 ▪ 4199 8538 ▪ www. hotelescubanacan.com ▪ $

A remodeled colonial townhouse on the edge of Parque Céspedes and the colonial quarter, it offers ample comfort in 14 air-conditioned rooms with mid-20th-century decor.

Hotel E Velasco, Matanzas

MAP E2 ▪ Calle Contreras 79 ▪ 4525 3880 ▪ www. hotelescubanacan.com ▪ $$

One of the only two hotels in Matanzas, this is set in a restored early 20th-century building on Parque Libertad. A small, boutique-style hotel, its rooms are attractively decorated. The restaurant is one of the better places to eat in town.

Hotel Mascotte, Remedios

MAP J2 ▪ Calle Máximo Gómez 114 ▪ 4239 5144 ▪ www.hotelescubana can.com ▪ $

This renovated historic hotel is situated just off the main plaza. All 10 rooms have modern bathrooms, and the restaurant is one of the best in town.

Hotel E Ordoño, Gibara

MAP P4 ▪ Calle J. Peralta between Marmól & Independencia ▪ 2484 5498 ▪ www.hoteles cubanacan.com ▪ $

Occupying a colonial mansion in the center of town, Ordoño features exquisite murals in its 21 rooms on two levels.

Hotel Terral, Centro Habana

MAP V1 ▪ Malecón & Lealtad ▪ www.gaviota hotels.com ▪ 7860 2100 ▪ $$

Opened in 2012, this is a stylish contemporary hotel that overlooks the Malecón, and has 14 spacious rooms, complete with modern amenities.

Horizontes Los Caneyes, Santa Clara

MAP H3 ▪ Av. de los Eucaliptos ▪ 4221 8140 ▪ www.hotelescubana can.com ▪ $$

Popular with tour groups, this hotel on the outskirts of town has comfortable, octagonal, thatched cabins with air conditioning and satellite TV. The elegant restaurant has buffet and à la carte meals. A pool-side fashion show is held each evening.

Private B&Bs and Room Rentals

Casa Menocal, Varadero

MAP F1 ▪ Calle 14 y Camino del Mar ▪ 5283 0269 ▪ vmoralesmeno cal1@gmail.com ▪ $

A private property on the beach, this 1940s family home offers five bedrooms. Break-fast and dinner can be arranged.

Casa Los Vitrales, Camagüey

MAP L3 ■ Calle Avellaneda 3 ■ 5294 2522 ■ $

An impressive colonial *casa* that was once a convent is set in the heart of the city. This spot is run by a friendly architect and his family. Featuring original wooden ceilings, large windows, and period furniture, all rooms are set around the inviting patio courtyard.

Hostal Girasol, Santiago de Cuba

MAP P6 ■ Calle Santa Rita (Diego Palacio) 409 ■ 2262 0513 ■ $

A wonderful family runs this seven-room *hostal*, painted with images of sunflowers. Breakfast is served on the roof terrace which offers unforgettable views of the city. Close to several city highlights, this is an ideal choice for those making their way to Santiago de Cuba.

Casa Colonial Muñoz, Trinidad

MAP H4 ■ Calle Martí 401 ■ 4199 3673 ■ www.casa. trinidadphoto.com ■ $

A spacious 18th-century home full of antiques is run by the knowledgeable and friendly Muñoz family, who speak English and can assist travelers. Each of the three bedrooms has a private bathroom. Delicious dinners are also served to guests.

Casa de Jorge Coalla, Havana

MAP T1 ■ Calle 1 456, Vedado ■ 7832 9032 ■ www.havanarooms rental.com ■ $

A friendly family hosts visitors in this two-room *casa particular* superbly located in Vedado close to key sites and a good choice of restaurants. The casa's spacious, air-conditioned rooms are well equipped, and the bathrooms have lots of hot water.

Casa Font, Trinidad

MAP H4 ■ Calle Gustavo Izquierdo 105 ■ 4199 3683 ■ www.casafont trinidad.jimdo.com ■ $

This 18th-century family home is furnished with Spanish colonial heirlooms. One of the guest rooms features an elegant bed decorated in mother-of-pearl. Friendly host Beatriz serves guests breakfast in the pretty patio garden.

Hostal Villa Lagarto, Cienfuegos

MAP G3 ■ Calle 35 no. 4B ■ 4366 1004 ■ hostal bahia@yahoo.es ■ $

Down on breezy Punta Gorda, this popular restaurant, with friendly staff, also offers stunning sea views and simple rooms on a terrace surrounded by hammocks and lush plants.

Hostal del Ángel, La Habana Vieja

MAP W4 ■ Calle Cuarteles 118 ■ 7863 6738 ■ www. pradocolonial.com ■ $$

This delightful, homely option is set in a restored colonial townhouse that's located on the edge of La Habana Vieja. Hostal del Ángel's elegant and classic period furnishings and high ceilings are a highlight, as are the balconies which offer great views of the city. There's a spiral staircase that leads to a library.

Hostal El Chalet, Remedios

MAP J2 ■ Calle Brigadier González 29 ■ 4239 6538 ■ jorgechalet@nauta.cu ■ $

This well-maintained 1950s home very close to the main square has two bedrooms. The one upstairs has a lounge, large bathroom, and an independent entrance. The other room has a smaller bathroom.

Villa Liba, Holguín

MAP N4 ■ Calle Maceo 46 ■ 2442 3823 ■ $

A short walk from both downtown and the Loma de Cruz, this 1950s house is owned by a well-educated, friendly couple. The two spacious guest rooms have period furnishings and are air-conditioned. Hearty meals are served on the patio. It has secure parking.

Casa Vitrales, La Habana Vieja

MAP W1 ■ Calle Habana 106 ■ 7866 2607 ■ www. cvitrales.com ■ $$

This exquisite private B&B, with nine rooms on three levels, sets a high standard with its eclectic yet stylish furnishings. Delicious breakfasts are served on the rooftop terrace.

Malecón 663, Centro Habana

MAP V1 ■ Centro Habana ■ 7860 1459 ■ www. malecon663.com ■ $$

Superbly located along the Malecón, close to several of Havana's top *paladares*, this seafront B&B has four individually-styled rooms. The rooftop bar hosts musicians and DJs nightly.

For a key to hotel price categories see p128

General Index

Acknowledgments

This edition updated by

Contributor Claire Boobbyer
Senior Editor Alison McGill
Senior Designer Vinita Venugopal
Project Editors Dipika Dasgupta, Zoë Rutland
Editor Nayan Keshan
Project Art Editor Bharti Karakoti
Picture Research Administrator Vagisha Pushp
Publishing Assistant Halima Mohammed
Jacket Designer Jordan Lambley
Cartographer Ashif
Cartography Manager Suresh Kumar
Senior DTP Designer Tanveer Zaidi
Senior Production Editor Jason Little
Senior Production Controller Samantha Cross
Deputy Managing Editor Beverly Smart
Managing Editors Shikha Kulkarni,
Hollie Teague
Managing Art Editor Sarah Snelling
Senior Managing Art Editor Priyanka Thakur
Art Director Maxine Pedliham
Publishing Director Georgeina Dee

DK would like to thank the following for their
contribution to the previous editions:
Christopher P. Baker, Matthew Norman,
Clare Peel, Hilary Bird, Ian O'Leary, Rough
Guides/Greg Roden, Tony Souter

The publisher would like to thank the
following for their kind permission to
reproduce their photographs:
(**Key:** a-above; b-below/bottom; c-centre;
f-far; l-left; r-right; t-top)

123RF.com: Greta Gabaglio 19tl.

4Corners: Werner Bertsch 22–3.

Alamy Stock Photo: Rubens Abboud
81clb; age fotostock, /Juan Muñoz 50crb, /
Toño Labra 51t; Arterra Picture Library /
van der Meer Marica 112t; Aurora Photos/
Beth Wald 89t; Sean David Baylis 65tr; Jens
Benninghofen 2tr, 34–5; Bildagentur-online/
Schickert 7tr, 78bl, 96tr; John Birdsall 57tr;
Blend Images/Jeremy Woodhouse 11br,
28crb, 31bl, 32bl; blickwinkel/McPHOTO/
SCO 98tl; Ian Bottle 39c; Nelly Boyd 55tl;
John Cairns 97b; Cephas Picture Agency/
Joris Luyten 81cra; Danita Delimont / Pete
Oxford 104tl; Tristan Deschamps 115tr; Dov
Makabaw Cuba 10crb, 60br, 66tl, 80tr, 106cla;
dpa picture alliance 52tl; Adam Eastland
79tl; epa european pressphoto agency b.v.
46ca; Everett Collection Historical 41tr;
F1online digitale Bildagentur GmbH/
Austrophoto 112br; tim gartside travel 12crb,
77tr; Astrid Harrisson 16br; hemis.fr/Patrick
Escudero 4b; Hemis.fr/ Patrick Frilet 99cr;
Ruth Hofshi 26cla; imageBROKER/Egon
Bömsch 72cla, /Peter Schickert 26bl;
INSADCO Photography/Martin Plöb 96clb;
J Marshall - Tribaleye Images 48tr, /World
Illustrated 40tl; Karol Kozlowski Premium
RM Collection 46tl; Vojko Kavcic 110ca;
Konstantin Kulikov 84tl; Lazyllama 17cra;
David Litschel 48bl; Melvyn Longhurst
111ca; Annette Lozinski 84cra; giovanni
mereghetti 106crb; Jill Meyer 44cra; Ian
Nellist 29bc; nobleIMAGES/Kate Noble
21tl; B. O'Kane 88crb; Anne-Marie Palmer
40cra, 73t; Sunshine Pics 104b, 105cla; Wolfi
Poelzer 18bl, 38bl, 87cla; Premaphotos 53bl;
robertharding 100–101; Ageev Rostislav 108bl;
Sagaphoto.com/Patrick Forget 85tl; Antony
Souter 47cl, 74b, 80cl, 109cl; Torontonian
58t; TravelMuse 107bl; Universal Images
Group/DeAgostini/W. Buss 10cla; Lucas
Vallecillos 2tl, 8–9; Westermann 49tr;
Poelzer Wolfgang 4crb, 24crb, 82–3, 88cla.

Bridgeman Images: 43tl; Jaime Abecasis
36b; Bibliotheque Nationale, Paris, /Archives
Charmet 37br.

Corbis: Phil Clarke Hill 67tr; Phil Clarke-Hill
49cl, 49bl; Destinations 63tl; epa/ Alejandro
Ernesto 69cl, 69tr; the food passionates/
Eva Gründemann 62cb; Patrick Frilet 3tl,
70–71; Wael Hamzeh 59tr; Hemis/Patrick
Frilet 60t; imageBROKER/ GTW 92cla, /
Hans Blossey 17tl; JAI/Walter Bibikow 4t,
65br; Frank Lukasseck 74cra; Radius
Images 62br; Bernard Radvaner 107tr;
Jose Fuste Raga 103cr; Reuters/Enrique
de la Osa 68tr; Robert Harding Picture
Library/Donald Nausbaum 61tr, /Michael
DeFreitas 53br; Paul Starosta 32tl; Greg
Stott 53cle; Jane Sweeney 94clb; Rodrigo
Torres 93tl; Vittorio Sciosia 61clb, 65cl.

Dreamstime.com: Adamico 3tr, 118-19;
Ansud 28cla; Kian Yung Chua 20–1;
Demerzel21 21br; Joan Egert 90cr; Stefano
Ember 12-13c; Filipe Frazao 10tr, 14–15;
Peng Ge 67cla, 75cl; Roxana González
47tr; Gudmund1 54clb; Hel080808 11cla;
Johann Helgason 90bl, Pablo Hidalgo 11cla,
26–7, Jedynakanna 7tl, 56tl; Jlabouyrie
32-33c; Juliorivalta 45bl; Kmiragaya 16cl,
24–25c, 42b, 58c, 64bl, 85br; Komposterblint
77cb; Konstik 16–17; Marco Lijoi 29tl; Daniel
Loncarevic 76b; Roberto Machado Noa
103tl; Nobohh 44cl; Christian Offenberg
4cra; Palino666 86bl; Natalia Pavlova
10clb; Carlos Perez 4clb; Matyas Rehak
102tl; Richard Semik 6cl, 11tr; Dubes
Sonego Junior 39tr; Nadezda Stoyanova
58bl; Rudolf Tepfenhart 10br; Aleksandar
Todorovic 4cla, 20br, 30cla, 55b, 113cla;
Tupungato 44bl; Sergey Uryadnikov 18cl,

24cla, 98crb; Venemama 50cla; Visualife 33tl; Wafuefotodesign 52br; John Ward 33bl, 86tr; Lena Wurm 63tr.

Getty Images: AFP/Adalberto Roque 27bc; Ulf Andersen 42tl; Günter Nindl 59cl; PHAS/UIG 36tr; Rolls Press/Popperfoto 37cla; Jane Sweeney 30clb.

Getty Images / iStock:
AutumnSkyPhotography 57cl; Robert Buchel 11cr; Diy13 4cl, 14bl; E+ / Eloi_Omella 1; E+ / golero 12bl; Jamie 111br; MaboHH 45tr; YinYang 66b; yykkaa 25crb.

Photoshot: World Pictures/Mel Longhurst 31cra.

Robert Harding Picture Library: Walter Bibikow 46br; Gunter Gruner 116t; Christopher Kimmel 24bl; Tono Labra 13tl; Juan Munoz 19cb; Ben Pipe 12cla; Ellen Rooney 15cr; Michael Runkel 30-1; Karl F. Schofmann 14cla; Jane Sweeney 20cl; Therin-Weise 18-19.

Shutterstock.com: Associated Newspapers 43br; Toms Auzins 64tl; Patrick Frilet 112br; Joaquin Hernandez 68b; imageBROKER 94t; Sovfoto/Universal Images Group 40bl; Underwood Archives/UIG 41clb.

Cover:

Front and spine: **Getty Images / iStock:** E+ / Eloi_Omella.

Back: **Dreamstime.com:** Anna Artamonova cl, Kmiragaya crb, Prillfoto tl, Vincentstthomas tr; **Getty Images / iStock:** E+ / Eloi_Omella b.

Pull Out Map Cover:

Getty Images / iStock: E+ / Eloi_Omella.

All other images © Dorling Kindersley
For further information see:
www.dkimages.com

Penguin Random House

First Edition 2008

Published in Great Britain by
Dorling Kindersley Limited
DK, One Embassy Gardens, 8 Viaduct
Gardens, London SW11 7BW, UK

The authorised representative in the EEA is
Dorling Kindersley Verlag GmbH. Arnulfstr.
124, 80636 Munich, Germany

Published in the United States by
DK Publishing, 1745 Broadway, 20th Floor,
New York, NY 10019, USA

Copyright © 2008, 2022
Dorling Kindersley Limited
A Penguin Random House Company

22 23 24 25 10 9 8 7 6 5 4 3 2 1

The publishers cannot accept responsibility
for any consequences arising from the use
of this book, nor for any material on third
party websites, and cannot guarantee that
any website address in this book will be a
suitable source of travel information.

A CIP catalog record is available from the
British Library

A catalog record for this book is available
from the Library of Congress

ISSN 1479-344X

ISBN 978-0-2415-6885-9

Printed and bound in Malaysia

www.dk.com

As a guide to abbreviations in visitor information blocks: **Adm** = admission charge; **D** = dinner.

MIX
Paper from
responsible sources
FSC™ C018179

This book was made with Forest
Stewardship Council ™ certified
paper – one small step in DK's
commitment to a sustainable future.
For more information go to
www.dk.com/our-green-pledge

Phrase Book

The Spanish spoken in Cuba is basically the same as the Castilian used in Spain with certain deviations. As in the Spanish-speaking countries in Central and Southern America, the "z" is pronounced like the "s", as is the "c" when it comes before "e" or "i." Among the grammatical variations, visitors should be aware that Cubans use *Ustedes* in place of *Vosotros*, to say "you" when referring to more than one person. It is notable that some Taíno, African, and English words are commonly used in present-day Cuban Spanish. This basic phrase book includes useful common phrases and words, and particular attention has been paid to typically Cuban idioms in a list of Cuban Terms.

Emergencies

Help!	*¡Socorro!*	sokorro
Stop!	*¡pare!*	pareh
Call a doctor	*Llamen a un médico*	yamen a oon medeeko
Call an ambulance	*Llamen a una ambulancia*	yamen a oona amboolans-ya
Police!	*¡Policía!*	poleesee-a
I've been robbed	*Me robaron*	meh robaron

Communication Essentials

Yes	*Sí*	see
No	*No*	no
Please	*Por favor*	por fabor
Pardon me	*Perdone*	pairdoneh
Excuse me	*Disculpe*	deeskoolpeh
I'm sorry	*lo siento*	lo s-yento
Thanks	*Gracias*	gras-yas
Hello!	*¡Buenas!*	bwenas
Good day	*Buenos días*	bwenos dee-as
Good afternoon	*Buenas tardes*	bwenas tardes
Good evening	*Buenas noches*	bwenas noches
night	*noche*	nocheh
morning	*mañana*	man-yana
tomorrow	*mañana*	man-yana
yesterday	*ayer*	a-yair
Here	*Acá*	aka
How?	*¿Cómo?*	komo
When?	*¿Cuándo?*	kwando
Where?	*¿Dónde?*	dondeh
Why?	*¿Por qué?*	por keh
How are you?	*¿Qué tal?*	keh tal
It's a pleasure!	*¡Mucho gusto!*	moocho goosto
Goodbye	*Hasta luego*	asta lwego

Useful Phrases

That's fine	*Está bien/ocá*	esta b-yen/oka
Fine	*¡Qué bien!*	keh b-yen
How long?	*¿Cuánto falta?*	kwanto falta
Do you speak a little English?	*¿Habla un poco de inglés?*	abla oon poko deh eengles
I don't understand	*No entiendo*	no ent-yendo
Could you speak more slowly?	*¿Puede hablar más despacio?*	pwedeh ablas mas despas-yo
I agree/ OK	*De acuerdo/ Ocá*	deh akwairdo/ oka
Certainly!	*¡Claro que sí!*	klaro keh see!
Let's go!	*¡Vámonos!*	bamonos

Useful Words

large	*grande*	grandeh
small	*pequeño*	peken-yo
hot	*caliente*	kal-yenteh
cold	*frío*	free-o
good	*bueno*	bweno
bad	*malo*	malo
well/fine	*bien*	b-yen
open	*abierto*	ab-yairto
closed	*cerrado*	serrado
full	*lleno*	yeno
empty	*vacío*	basee-o
right	*derecha*	dairecha
left	*izquierda*	isk-yairda
straight	*recto*	rekto
under	*debajo*	debaho
over	*arriba*	arreeba
quickly/ early	*pronto/ temprano*	pronto/ temprano
late	*tarde*	tardeh
now	*ahora*	a-ora
delay	*demora*	deh-mora
more	*más*	mas
less	*menos*	menos
little	*poco*	poko
sufficient	*suficiente*	soofees-yenteh
much	*mucho/muy*	moocho/mwee
too much	*demasiado*	demas-yado
in front of	*delante*	delanteh
behind	*detrás*	detras
first floor	*primer piso*	preemair peeso
ground floor	*planta baja*	planta baha
lift/elevator	*elevador*	elebador
bathroom/toilet	*servicios baños*	sairbees-yos ban-yos
women	*mujeres*	moohaires
men	*hombres*	ombres
toilet paper	*papel sanitario*	papel saneetar-yo
camera	*cámara*	kamara
batteries	*baterías*	batairee-as
passport	*pasaporte*	pasaporteh
visa; tourist card	*visa; tarjeta turística*	beesa; tarheta tooreesteeka

Transport

Could you call a taxi for me?	*¿Me puede llamar a un taxi?*	meh pwedeh yamar a oon taksee?
airport	*aeropuerto*	a-airopwairto
train station	*estación de ferrocarriles*	estas-yon deh fairrokarreeles
bus station	*terminal de guagua*	tairmeenal deh gwa-gwa
When does it leave?	*¿A qué hora sale?*	a keh ora saleh?
customs	*aduana*	adwana
boarding pass	*tarjeta de embarque*	tarheta deh embarkeh
car hire	*alquiler de carros*	alkeelair deh karros
bicycle	*bicicleta*	beeseekleta
insurance	*seguro*	segooro
petrol/gas station	*la gasolinera*	la gasoleenaira

Staying in a Hotel

single room/ double	*habitación sencilla/ doble*	*abeetas-yon sensee-ya /dobleh*
shower	*ducha*	*doocha*
bathtub	*bañera*	*ban-yaira*
balcony	*balcón, terraza*	*balkon, tairrasa*
warm water	*agua caliente*	*agwa kal-yenteh*
cold water	*agua fría*	*agwa free-a*
soap	*jabón*	*habon*
towel	*toalla*	*to-a-ya*
key	*llave*	*yabeh*

Eating Out

What is there to eat?	*¿Qué hay para comer?*	*keh I para komair?*
The bill please	*La cuenta por favor*	*la kwenta por fabor*
I would like some water	*Quisiera un poco de agua*	*kees-yaira oon poko deh agwa*
Do you have wine?	*¿Tienen vino?*	*t-yenen beeno?*
The beer is not cold enough	*La cerveza no está bien fría*	*la sairbesa no esta b-yen free-a*
breakfast	*desayuno*	*desa-yoono*
lunch	*almuerzo*	*almwairso*
dinner	*comida*	*komeeda*
raw/cooked	*crudo/cocido*	*kroodo/ koseedo*
glass	*vaso*	*baso*
cutlery	*cubiertos*	*koob-yairtos*

Menu Decoder

aceite	*asayteh*	oil
agua mineral	*agwa meenairal*	mineral water
aguacate	*agwakateh*	avocado
ajo	*aho*	garlic
arroz	*arros*	rice
asado	*asado*	roasted
atún	*atoon*	tuna
azúcar	*asookar*	sugar
bacalao	*bakala-o*	cod
café	*kafeh*	coffee
camarones	*kamarones*	prawns
carne	*karneh*	meat
cerveza	*sairbesa*	beer
congrí	*kongree*	rice with beans and onions
dulce	*doolseh*	sweet, dessert
ensalada	*ensalada*	salad
fruta	*froota*	fruit
fruta bomba	*froota bomba*	papaya
helado	*elado*	ice cream
huevo	*webo*	egg
jugo	*hoogo*	fruit juice
langosta	*langosta*	lobster
leche	*lecheh*	milk
mantequilla	*mantekee-ya*	butter
marisco	*mareesko*	seafood
pan	*pan*	bread
papas	*papas*	potatoes
pescado	*peskado*	fish
plátano	*platano*	banana
pollo	*po-yo*	chicken
postre	*postreh*	dessert
potaje/sopa	*potaheh/sopa*	soup
puerco cerdo	*pwairko serrdo*	pork
queso	*keso*	cheese
refresco	*refresko*	drink
sal	*sal*	salt
salsa	*salsa*	sauce
té	*teh*	tea
vinagre	*beenagreh*	vinegar

Cuban Terms

apagón	*apagon*	black-out, power outage
babalawo	*babala-wo*	a priest of Afro-Cuban religion
batey	*batay*	village around sugar factory
carro	*karro*	car
casa de la trova	*kasa deh la troba*	traditional music venue
cayo	*ka-yo*	small island
chama	*chama*	child
criollo	*kr-yo-yo*	Creole (born in Cuba of Spanish descent)
divisas	*deebeesas*	hard currency
eva	*eba*	woman
guagua	*gwagwa*	bus
guajiro	*gwaheero*	farmer
guarapo	*gwarapo*	sugar cane juice
ingenio	*eenhen-yo*	sugar factory complex
jama	*hama*	food, meal
jinetera	*heenetaira*	prostitute, or female hustler
jinetero	*heenetairo*	male person hustling tourists
libreta	*leebreta*	rations book
moneda libremente convertible MLC	*moneda leebramentey converteebley*	freely convertible currency
moneda nacional	*moneda nas-yonal*	pesos ("national currency")
moros y cristianos	*moros ee krist-yanos*	rice and black beans
paladar	*paladar*	privately owned restaurant
puro	*pooro*	Cuban cigar
santero	*santairo*	santería priest
tabaco	*tabako*	low-quality cigar
tienda	*t-yenda*	shop
trago	*trago*	alcoholic drink
tunas	*toonas*	prickly pears
zafra	*safra*	sugarcane harvest

Health

I don't feel well	*Me siento mal*	*meh s-yento mal*
I have a…	*Me duele…*	*meh dweleh…*
stomach ache	*el estómago*	*el estomago*
headache	*la cabeza*	*la kabesa*
He/she is ill	*Está enfermo/a*	*esta enfairmo*
I need to rest	*Necesito*	*neseseeto*
	decansar	*dekansar*
drug store	*farmacia*	*farmasee-ya*

Post Office and Bank

bank	*banco*	*banko*
I want to send	*Quiero enviar*	*k-yairo emb-yar*
a letter	*una carta*	*oona karta*
postcard	*postal tarjeta*	*postal tarheta*
stamp	*sello*	*se-yo*
draw out money	*sacar dinero*	*sakar deenairo*

Shopping

How much is it?	*¿Cuánto cuesta?*	*kwanto kwesta*
What time do you open/ close?	*¿A qué hora abre/cierra?*	*a ke ora abreh/ s-yairra*
May I pay with a credit card?	*¿Puedo pagar con tarjeta de crédito?*	*pwedo pagar kon tarheta deh kredeeto?*

Sightseeing

beach	*playa*	*pla-ya*
castle, fortress	*castillo*	*kastee-yo*
cathedral	*catedral*	*katedral*
church	*iglesia*	*eegles-ya*
district	*barrio*	*barr-yo*
garden	*jardín*	*hardeen*
guide	*guía*	*gee-a*
house	*casa*	*kasa*
motorway	*autopista*	*owtopeesta*
museum	*museo*	*mooseh-o*
park	*parque*	*parkeh*
road	*carretera*	*karretaira*
square, plaza	*plaza, parque*	*plasa, parkeh*
street	*calle, callejón*	*ka-ye, ka-yehon*
town hall	*Ayuntamiento*	*a-yoontam-yento*
tourist bureau	*buró de turismo*	*booro deh tooreesmo*
Can I take a picture?	*Puedo sacar una foto?*	*pwedo sack-arr sacko oon-a photo de oo-sted?*
Do you mind if I take your picture?	*Le molesta si saco una foto de usted?*	*Ley mol-esta see sacko oon-a photo de oo-sted?*

Numbers

0	*cero*	*sairo*
1	*uno*	*oono*
2	*dos*	*dos*
3	*tres*	*tres*
4	*cuatro*	*kuatro*
5	*cinco*	*seenko*
6	*seis*	*says*
7	*siete*	*s-yeteh*
8	*ocho*	*ocho*
9	*nueve*	*nwebeh*
10	*diez*	*d-yes*
11	*once*	*onseh*
12	*doce*	*doseh*
13	*trece*	*treseh*
14	*catorce*	*katorseh*
15	*quince*	*keenseh*
16	*dieciséis*	*d-yeseesays*
17	*diecisiete*	*d-yesees-yeteh*
18	*dieciocho*	*d-yesee-yocho*
19	*diecinueve*	*d-yeseenwebeh*
20	*veinte*	*baynteh*
30	*treinta*	*traynta*
40	*cuarenta*	*kwarenta*
50	*cincuenta*	*seenkwenta*
60	*sesenta*	*sesenta*
70	*setenta*	*setenta*
80	*ochenta*	*ochenta*
90	*noventa*	*nobenta*
100	*cien*	*s-yen*

Time

minute	*minuto*	*meenooto*
hour	*hora*	*ora*
half-hour	*media hora*	*med-ya ora*
Monday	*lunes*	*loones*
Tuesday	*martes*	*martes*
Wednesday	*miércoles*	*m-yairkoles*
Thursday	*jueves*	*hwebes*
Friday	*viernes*	*b-yairnes*
Saturday	*sábado*	*sabado*
Sunday	*domingo*	*domeengo*
January	*enero*	*enairo*
February	*febrero*	*febrairo*
March	*marzo*	*marso*
April	*abril*	*abreel*
May	*mayo*	*ma-yo*
June	*junio*	*hoon-yo*
July	*julio*	*hool-yo*
August	*agosto*	*agosto*
September	*septiembre*	*sept-yembreh*
October	*octubre*	*oktoobreh*
November	*noviembre*	*nob-yembreh*
December	*diciembre*	*dees-yembreh*